7

9

# A CAPTAIN'S RANSOM

# A CAPTAIN'S RANSOM

Captain Alexander 'Joe' Westland

The Book Guild Ltd

First published in Great Britain in 2017 by
The Book Guild Ltd
9 Priory Business Park
Wistow Road, Kibworth
Leicestershire, LE8 0RX
Freephone: 0800 999 2982
www.bookguild.co.uk
Email: info@bookguild.co.uk
Twitter: @bookguild

Typeset in Minion Pro

Printed and bound in Great Britain by CPI Group (UK) Ltd, Croydon, CR0 4YY

ISBN 978 1912083 671

British Library Cataloguing in Publication Data.
A catalogue record for this book is available from the British Library.

*To Chris Woolley, who was my boss at the time and MD Of PW Marine Ltd. He was the one that negotiated with pirates etc and came up with the cash to secure my release.*

*Also to Alabo and Omini, they were the ones that volunteered and put their own lives at risk to meet with the kidnappers, without any protection in the dead of night, with a large sum of money, again to secure my release.*

# CONTENTS

# ACKNOWLEDGEMENTS

In May 2013, I was kidnapped by pirates whilst working off the coast of Nigeria. I was taken at gunpoint to a jungle hut where I was held captive for four days. I felt sure that nobody would ever find me. It was the most horrifying event of my life.

I have written this book for many reasons. Firstly, I hope it helps in my recovery from a terrible personal ordeal. Secondly, I want to thank all those well-wishers who have given me tremendous support since my return home. My family and friends in Scotland all know about my ordeal but have not yet heard the full story. I have written this book so they might understand what I went through, and why I am afraid to return to work in Nigeria.

I am indebted to my good friends and work colleagues who played a vital role in my rescue and have helped in my ongoing recovery. I will start with Chris Woolley, my dear friend and the managing director of PW Resources. He dealt with the pirates, carried out negotiations, and he found a large amount of cash in a short period of time to save my life. He also had to ask another of my two good friends and colleagues, Omini and Alabo, to undertake great personal risk and carry out the handover of cash in return for my life. Thank you very much, Chris, Omini and Alabo.

I would like thank my dear wife Helen, who has been my strength since returning home. On numerous occasions she has reassured me, saying: "You are here, you are safe and have a second chance at life, so live it to its full." I would also like to thank my daughter, Tracey, and my grandchildren, David (Shimmy), Dean and Darcie. They have been a great help to me. I also owe a debt of gratitude to my brother, Roy, and his wife, Evelyn, who looked after Helen and me during the first weekend after I returned home. I would also like to thank Helens sister Irene, and Alan, my brother-in-law, for all their support. Thank you all.

I would also like to acknowledge my appreciation for a special group of friends. I will not go into detail but the people I am going to mention will never know how much help they have been to me in lots of various ways. They are: Kenny Kemp, Roger Hunt, John Stewart, Audrey, June MacDonald, Paul Partridge and Ken Mackie. Thank you all very much indeed. I will never forget you and the support you have given Helen and I since our ordeal.

I want to thank Jim Hampton too. After my ordeal, I went fly-fishing for the first time at Rescobie Loch, near Forfar. Here, the small boats reminded me of the vessels the kidnappers used to take me from the St Patrick and I began shaking uncontrollably. Jim calmed me down, told me that I would be OK and we eventually went out on the boat and tried to catch a few trout. Thank you very much indeed, Jim. A massive thank you also goes to Phil Lamb, who has been a tower of strength and helped me tremendously in my recovery. I appreciate everything you have done, Phil.

Alabo and Omini ignored the risk to their own lives and volunteered to take a large sum of money in a plastic bag through two Nigerian villages in the dark of night, and then took a hired boat into the open sea to meet with my attackers to exchange money for my release. This is something that I will never forget for the rest of my life and I will be forever grateful.

I am so very grateful to be back in Scotland, a wonderful country that we often take for granted.

# FOREWORD

My work off the coast of West Africa, particularly east of the Niger delta, has been good to me and my family. Firstly, it has given us a comfortable lifestyle and, secondly, I have met many remarkable people who have become firm friends. I knew very little about Ghana, the Ivory Coast or Nigeria and the different cultures and customs of these countries before I began working there more than 12 years ago.

In the early years, it was relatively safe but over the last few years the country has become an extremely dangerous place to live and work for European expatriates. In my opinion, I believe this is a symptom of the nation's broken society. The international oil industry has made Nigeria an extremely rich nation but it is a society where the rule of law is not evident. Most of the money from the oil industry has been siphoned off to the Nigerian government and an elite clique of people in power. The ordinary Nigerian gets very little from the government. Yet the levels of poverty in the country simply do not equate to how much money the Nigerian government has received from the crude oil that is pumped out of Nigerian waters. Let's remember the nation gets 60%, while the international oil companies get 40% and have to pay all the expenses to get the oil to the consumer.

A stark example of the Nigerian government's neglect is the unimaginable piles of rubbish that are dumped on the streets, due to an absence of bins, and left to rot in the sun. There are also no public toilets, so the homeless go into the bush to do the toilet. They wash in mosquito-infested water and have no towels to dry themselves. The number of poor people begging on the streets for food is a crying shame. It is understandable why ordinary Nigerians resent their government, and the white Westerners they perceive as exploiting their oil. Few Nigerians have a good word to say about their leaders. The poor are also mistreated by the police and, as a result, seldom experience fair justice. Beatings and killings are daily occurrences in Nigeria, yet the police authorities do little or nothing. I have met hundreds of Nigerians, both poor and rich, and none of them have anything good to say about the rulers of their country. Life has become cheap in much of Africa. That is hard for a European to fully understand. Killing and murder are common place, and go on with impunity. Up until my capture, I enjoyed my time in Nigeria and worked with great Nigerian guys from various tribes. But, like every segment of life, there are bad elements.

After two days in captivity I made some key decisions which I now believe saved my life. Hostage-taking experts told me later that my actions and quick thinking certainly helped to get me out of the jungle alive. This story is about these actions but it is also a warning to others We all want to do things in life to better ourselves and our families but often we are unaware of the dangers and consequences. I was certainly unaware of what could happen in Nigeria at the offset. Many people have questioned whether ex-pats should be in Nigeria in the first place. However, if you are a Merchant Seaman like me and are used to working away from home for many months at a time, it is simply part of the job and trouble is something you tend to put to the back of your mind.

There are hot spots around the world yet, in my opinion, there is seldom enough warning given out by the British Government about the dangers of working in Nigeria. After my incident I browsed the internet for information on piracy. I discovered that the US Government continuously issue warnings to its citizens about the hazards in West and East Africa. I recall the British High Commission issuing a warning some years ago, stating that if British citizens went to work in Nigeria, they did so at their own risk. That has been the sum of it. Personally, I don't recall any further warnings after this. So this is my personal warning to you: Nigeria is dangerous. I know British and Irish people who have been killed. One Irish engineer called Robert Gray from Westport in Mayo was ambushed and shot dead in August 2012 near the town of Takum, close to the Cameroon border. I feel desperately sorry for Robert's family, yet we all take calculated risks thinking that nothing is going to happen to us. Maybe we are too blasé? I know there are expats from the UK and Ireland working in Nigeria without fully appreciating the terrible risks.

My kidnap and the aftermath were truly terrifying. Throughout my days in captivity, I was waiting and mentally preparing to be executed. I was kidnapped by machine-gun totting pirates and threatened with my life. The full horror of the attack and my kidnapping still haunt me. There is not a day goes by that I do not think about what happened. I see the angry faces and the guns in my sleep, and even when I am driving or going fishing. It was and still is my worst nightmare.

I hope by reading this story you will understand my ordeal. I do not know if things will ever be normal again. For me, recounting this story is part of my own recovery. If you are an ex-pat going to work in Nigeria, bear in mind that you will need to be escorted by armed Nigerian police or private security people. It is no longer a place for the faint-hearted, so, if you're going to live and work there, please take care.

# 1

# THE SEA

The sea has been my life. I am now 64 (June 2014) and have been a sea captain for over 30 years. It has given me a decent living and, in return, I have always given the sea my utmost respect. My constant yardstick has been keeping my vessel, my crew and myself safe. In May 2013 I was master of the *St Patrick*, a special-purpose crane barge, operating in the waters off the coast of Nigeria. The Qua Iboe oilfields are just over 4 degrees north of the equator, so it is an area of intense tropical heat, particularly at the height of the day on the deck of an unshaded construction crane barge.

I have a fading tattoo on my left arm which has the name of the first fishing vessel that I worked on out of Aberdeen – the *Glenisla*. I had it done in 1965 in a back street tattoo parlour close to Aberdeen harbour when I was just 15. I thought it looked gallous but my skipper, James Alex Simpson, a God-fearing man from Buckie, on the north-east coast of Scotland, was not impressed. He told me I was foolish to be marked for life like this, but what he did not realise was that the tattoo was intended as a tribute to him and his vessel.

I left school in Aberdeen at 15 and went straight to the local training school for fishermen. It was after this I started as a trainee deck-hand with skipper Simpson on the *Glenisla*. It was a brutal baptism in the heavy seas and bone-numbing chill of the North Sea. Skipper Simpson taught me a great deal about survival in this hostile environment, and I have carried this knowledge with me every day since then. He instilled in me the ethos that a good seaman takes nothing for granted and that a skipper is the master at sea. He must always keep an eye out for changing circumstances, watch the weather, the changing sea condition and the horizon. Above all, he said a skipper's overriding concern is for the safety of the vessel and its crew. A skipper has to be like a father to his crew at times and guide his crew in the right direction on deck, he also has to teach his crew the basics of navigation, weather forecasts. A skipper's duty is to catch fish for the owners and obviously for himself and his crew to provide a good salary for their families. Moreover, safety on a fishing trawler is paramount as a lot of dangerous things take place on the deck of a fishing trawler. The fishing nets, wires and chains, go into the water at great speeds, so the crews have to be alert and very careful at all times, especially in poor weather conditions. This is where the skipper's wisdom comes into play, he passes on his expertise to the chief officer on deck, who then looks after the crew and the skipper's interests.

A master of a fishing vessel is commonly known as a skipper and a master of a Merchant Navy vessel is normally called the master or captain.

I became a skipper in my late twenties regularly working in challenging weather conditions and high seas, bringing in cod, haddock and whiting for the dining tables of Britain. I worked in the Scottish fishing industry until it was forced into a decline in the 70s. The fish quotas and number of days allowed at sea for deep sea trawlers became too much of a challenge for trawler owners. This had a greater effect in the Scottish sector for some reason, as most of the English trawler owners took their vessels back to England whilst, concurrently, many Scottish trawler owners lost their vessels through a government decommissioning scheme. This heralded the beginning of the end for deep sea trawlers in Aberdeen. However, I have always kept Captain Simpson's words of wisdom in mind.

As the fishing industry was waning, the North Sea oil industry began to boom, and there was money to be made, so in 1980 I went to work offshore on a BP oil platform – the *Forties Bravo*. My brother had always told me that working for BP was very good in terms of salary, pension and other benefits, and when I was offered the job by BP it was not a hard decision to make. Working on platforms would turn out to be a huge difference to working at sea on trawlers and Merchant Navy vessels. Of course there was a huge difference between working on deep sea trawlers and working on Merchant Navy vessels. I was no longer the boss, but was instead taking orders from other people, which was something I had not done for many years. But after 7 happy years working offshore I was badly injured in an accident, which forced me to spend some time ashore, and I eventually returned to the Merchant Navy as a first mate of a standby vessel, operating out of Montrose. After a while, I was offered offshore work in Africa. It seemed so exotic and as I was in my early 50s, I thought operating in the tropical seas off Ghana and Nigeria, where the weather conditions were a lot friendlier than the weather conditions in the North Sea, would make for a welcome change.

In May 2013, I was Master on the *St Patrick*, a special purpose DP2 crane barge working off the Nigerian coast of West Africa. The DP stands for 'dynamic positioning', which means that the vessel's engines and thrusters are connected to a computer in the wheel house. I could put the vessel in any position and then lock that position into the computer, keeping the vessel in an exact location allows materials and heavy gear to be loaded and unloaded from other vessels and platforms. The system is also used for commercial diving operations. I was the only expat on board with a native crew of Nigerians. Most had been with me for several years and called me 'father'.

The crew were a mix of different African ethnic minorities and tribes often hostile to one another onshore, but on board my vessel I had them all working as a team. We were there to concentrate on the job in hand. While my job is to help make money for the company, I was fully committed to keeping my crew as safe as possible.

When I was kidnapped my vessel was off-hire and at anchor as we were awaiting spare parts to arrive for our Manitowoc 888 deck crane. The crane with its caterpillar tracks has a heavy lifting capacity of 230 tons, with a cab at the front. It is secured by hefty chains onto the deck of the barge.

It was another sweltering tropical day with azure blue skies above and a shimmering haze on the inky-blue water. The sun was baking the metal surfaces on our deck on which you could fry an egg if you were so inclined. We were up early after dawn to avoid the full furnace of this tropical heat. I was in the wheelhouse supervising the auto controls of the DP system. A massive fan was whirring away, trying to keep us cool, but my T-shirt was still soaked with sweat. We were on station on DP alongside one of Exxon Mobil's supply vessels. The oil giants BP have been operating in the Qua Iboe oil fields since 1970, working in conjunction with the Nigerian National Petroleum Corporation (NNPC), which holds a 60% share on behalf of the government. Light crude oil has been a bountiful fount of Nigeria's wealth.

It was then that our crane broke down. Little did we know then but the crane breaking down was the first thing in a chain of events that would later play a big part in the vessel being attacked and me being kidnapped and held hostage for ransom money. If the crane had not broken down then we would still have been working and would not have been exposed whilst lying at anchor in the same location every night for two weeks. If the vessel moves from anchorage to anchorage each night it becomes a lot more difficult for the pirates to keep track of the vessel. Most of the safe anchorages in the middle of the Exxon Mobil field have several security vessels in attendance at night, but because we chose the Idoho safe anchorage for better communications and to make it easier logistically for the company, we were at a greater risk, and the crane breaking down was obviously our initial downfall.

I was looking out the window and watched the crane operator lifting a heavy container from our deck. I heard a shout of 'Keep Clear!' and suddenly the massive 220ft boom started to shudder and come down swiftly on its own. The crane driver jammed on the emergency boom brake, but the boom continued to come down, only much slower. Thankfully, the operator was a skilled guy and managed to place the container back on the supply vessel's deck. I picked up the short-wave radio and called the other captain, requesting him to instruct his deck crew to unhook the container immediately, and go full steam ahead with his vessel to avoid the crane boom from crashing down on his vessel.

This was a very dicey situation, but it was important to remain calm. There was a danger of causing serious injury or death and very serious damage, unless everyone was careful and followed my instructions. We were very fortunate indeed that no injuries or damages were sustained. This was one situation where being cool calm and collected came into play; panic in this instance would have been a disaster. My chief officer said later, "Cap, you were wonderful. I dread to think what would have happened if you had not been here, you stayed very calm and did not get flustered." Little did he know that inside I had the same concerns as everyone else, but as captain you take it in your stride as you have to stay calm for everyone's sake. When I think of what could have happened it is very scary, people could have been killed, and, at best, the supply vessel could have been badly damaged, or could have been sunk if the load had come down with force. Without blowing my own trumpet, I think making the right decisions and staying calm in this situation was imperative and may well have saved lives.

With the imminent danger over, it was now the engineer's task to get the crane boom back on our deck. However, the crane jib was still in a very precarious position. The jib was now lying over the ship's side by 180 feet and resting on our hand rail that was now buckled. I immediately contacted Exxon Mobil and spoke to the onshore marine coordinator for Exxon's shore base at Eket, to make them aware of the situation. He was responsible for keeping track of our work. I then called my own company to inform them. Meanwhile, Dimitrij Manastirlic, our Croatian chief engineer, worked on the crane all day with his engineering officers trying to fix the crane but to no avail. In the evening, after a long telephone conversation with Chris Woolley, my managing director, it was agreed I should move the vessel to a safe anchorage until the crane was back in action. I steered the vessel at a very slow speed – just 4 knots – towards the Idaho North Safe Anchorage, one of Exxon's dedicated safe anchorages with a security vessel in attendance at all times. This anchorage was approximately 11 miles off the coast where Exxon are based. I was annoyed that the Manitowoc crane had broken down but in the 11 years that I had served as master of this vessel the crane had never let us down before. It was reliable, serviced every six months and all its certificates were up to date. But this lull gave me an opportunity to catch up with other work that sometimes cannot be done whilst the vessel is on hire. I have always taken pride in making sure that my vessels are in the best condition possible. Even when a ship is idle I am busy arranging its daily upkeep, and ensuring its maintenance, paintwork and repairs are up to date. There are always crew safety equipment checks, lifeboat drills etc. at least once a week and mostly on a Sunday. This was all part of the ebb and flow of our lives at sea. As the day cooled and night set in, I stood on the bridge wing of the *St Patrick* puffing on my favourite St Moritz menthol cigarette. It was a contemplative moment for me in the late evening as I cast my gaze to the coastline from our current location of the Idoho safe anchorage. I knew that onshore in some of those jungle creeks there was a growing resentment and anger at the Westerners who were stealing 'their' oil. The jungle drums must have been beating. Through the grapevine, local pirates heard that I was alone and a sitting duck. In some dark eyes, I was fair game in the growing epidemic of international piracy and kidnapping that is making the seas off West Africa dangerous and unsafe for expatriates. On this starlit night I could see the silhouette of the jungle and the tiny flickers of open fires and electric lights in some of the coastal settlements on the estuary. Here, there are close knit communities of Ijaw, Ikwerre, Edo Itiskeri, Urhobo, Isoko, Ndoni, Andoni, Ibibio, Etache and Ogoni tribes dotted along the shore. I knew each tribe was fiercely proud and ethnic violence and tension was never far from the surface.

As the days passed after the breakdown of the crane, I was increasingly frustrated by the apparent lack of urgency from the suppliers in getting the parts to us. The parts were quite large and very important to the working of the crane boom hoist. The boom hoist clutch had shattered into several pieces and could not be repaired so had to be replaced. The boom hoist clutch was basically the part that made the crane hoist go up and down. The boom hoist brake motor was also damaged beyond repair this was what had caused the boom hoist to come down on its own whilst we were carrying out the container lifts with the supply vessel. The manufacturer of the crane is Manitowoc, who are based in America and they did not have the parts on the shelves, which meant they took a long time to arrive.

While waiting I made my normal VHF radio checks with Exxon, the Idoho Platform and the Onshore Marine Coordinator. The onshore marine coordinator is basically in control of all the vessels operating in the Exxon Mobil Nigeria field. Every task we undertook had to be reported daily to the

OMC. We also had to let them know twice daily how much fuel, water and other essentials we had on board. All the vessels working for Exxon had to do this, sometimes you had to stand by your radio for an hour to get your turn to give your report. We also had to report our evening position to the OMC every night, this way they knew exactly where all the vessels were all the time.

On Saturday, 11th May 2013, the radio buzzed and I heard the familiar African accent of the Exxon Mobil Marine Coordinator.

"Calling Captain Alex on the *St Patrick*. Have you seen or heard anything untoward or unusual? Over."

"*St Patrick* here. No, it's all quiet here. Over," I replied.

"Well, we have had reports of pirate activity in the area from one of the security vessels. We have also heard reports of shots being fired in your area, anything like that near you? Over."

"We have not heard or seen anything untoward here. As I say, all quiet over here."

"Captain Alex, make sure you are all locked up at night and your watch keepers keep a good look out and report anything suspicious. Over and out."

"OK, thank you for the warning. Over and out."

I passed this information on to all the crew on board and briefed them all again as to what to do if the vessel was attacked. They were all aware of the emergency procedures as we had emergency drills and pirate attack drills once a week. I always chaired the security drills as I held my S.S.O. (Ships Security Officer) certificate. I obtained this certificate at college where I covered vessel security, kidnapping and the attack of vessels in depth. Most vessel officers have to have this certificate now, but all we could really do on board was to make sure everything was locked up and make it as difficult as possible for any intruders to get to us. The emergency drills we had practiced were clearly effective, as the only way the pirates would gain access to the vessel would be by smashing the bridge windows.

That night I wasn't unduly worried – in hindsight perhaps I should have been. I finished doing my paperwork, including the crew's travel expenses for the upcoming crew change. I typed out a goodnight email to Helen back home in Scotland.

*"Hi Helen, Been a quiet day and again rather warm. We're still waiting for the spare part for the crane. Hope you've had a good day – I'm looking forward to seeing you soon. Love. Joe."*

I was also preoccupied by thoughts about my crew and the daily issues that we faced. My chief officer was Erik, a Nigerian who now lives in Russia. This was Erik's second stint with me, and he was very good at his job. A good trustworthy officer who did most things well but for some reason he was always arguing with the onshore office about his shifts and time off. On this trip, he had agreed to join the vessel and do an eight-week tour but when the crane broke down there was not so much for him to do and he told me that he wanted to go home. I discussed this with Chris the MD who said Erik was not going anywhere. He had agreed to do a full trip and would be paid for this. That was that. I passed this message to Erik and he did not like it. He told me he was having domestic problems and needed to get away. For me, it was simply an excuse as Erik had previously tried a similar thing with Captain Bob. Captain Bob told me that he had problems with Erik in the past. Erik would sign up for a period of time but get fed up before he had run his time and want home early. Bob's view was that as Erik also had a Master's certificate he liked giving out orders but didn't really like taking them. I began to realise a number of our crew did not get on with Erik. One day I heard a lot of shouting on the deck and wondered what all the commotion was. Later that day a delegation from the crew came to see me on the bridge and complained. I dismissed their issues, backing Erik, and saying he was Chief Officer on board and that they had to respect his position. In my view, the rules and responsibilities at sea are different from the normal ways of working in an office. The officer is always right, or so it goes.

Erik called Chris to complain about his decision, telling him he wanted to go home. Chris reluctantly agreed that Erik could go home as soon as a replacement arrived. Increasingly, Erik was becoming a major pain in the backside and it looked like his chances of working with us again were not good. If he left us now, then I couldn't see a way back for him. One of our chief engineers was a Nigerian called Victor Nwachukwu, who lived with his family in Port Harcourt. He joined us two years earlier while the vessel was in dry dock in Abidjan. Victor was hired to assist the engineering specialist to install and test the new engines and generators. Victor turned out to be an excellent engineer with a deep knowledge and understanding of marine engines. He was a very conscientious and hardworking man. After the spell in dry dock, the former chief engineer who worked back-to-back with Dimitri decided to leave and so Victor was promoted to Chief. This was an excellent choice. Victor would do anything he could for me, and always with a smile on his face, at least until the crane broke down. I have never seen anything get the better of him but we found out later that two of the crane parts were un-repairable so nobody could have fixed them. Thompson, the second engineer, was also a Nigerian citizen. After myself, Thompson was the longest serving crew member of the *St Patrick*. He wasn't the best of engineers but was reliable if there was ever a problem with the engines or generators. He would be there to assist until the job was completed and do anything that he was told or shown. Thompson was very popular with the crew and the office staff, and we had a very good relationship. Like most of the crew, he called me his father, although in reality I was not that much older than him.

The catering department consisted of a camp boss, who was in charge of the catering; a continental cook, for the expats; a national cook, for the local crew; and three stewards, one assigned to the galley, one to the upper accommodation and one for the lower accommodation and the new accommodation, which were Portakabins on the deck. Some of them had been with me for a long time, and they were all very good and hard workers. The vessel was always kept as clean as possible. The stewards would change every bed once per week. This was a big job when we had a full complement of 60 personnel on board.

Nde, the camp boss, had been with me for quite some time and joined as a continental cook before we promoted him to Camp Boss. As I was on the wheelhouse most of the time, Nde would cook and bring my meals to the bridge. He was always happy to oblige.

On the deck we had a Quarter master, the Third Hand, and four ABs or deckhands. The deck crew had also been with me for a long time. Two of the guys joined the vessel some years before with no qualifications. Bob and I managed to get them up to scratch. We might have to tell them to do something several times before they understood and did what was required. Two of the ABs, Obinna and Frankie, stuck together like glue and would often give me a headache with their antics. They were a right pair but turned out to be very good workers, when I could get them to work that is. They both came from Port Harcourt and had young families. Earlier that day Obinna came to me and told me he was suffering from stomach pains, although the medic did not think it was serious. However, Obinna insisted that he wanted to see a doctor and he was sent ashore in a small boat that had brought us food supplies and bottled water. We also carried an electrician. We had one expat, John Base, who was on leave and his back-to-back position was taken by a local lad called King Benard. King was in his early thirties and had also been with me for a long time. Benard and Bob didn't get on very well either. Bob thought Benard was lazy and useless as an electrician: Bob and I agreed to differ regarding this. So it was an experienced Nigerian crew on board that evening – many guys that I knew extremely well.

On the Sunday night Nde, the camp boss, brought my

supper to my cabin and we chatted for a few minutes about how the day had gone. Then I did my rounds with the second officer and made sure that the vessel was all locked up and that we were as secure as possible. I went to the bridge wing again to have another cigarette. It was a balmy evening and all seemed very peaceful. I said goodnight to the watch keepers and told them if there was any problems to give me a call. This was the normal Master's night orders. There was a night order book that all watch keepers signed every night to acknowledge the written orders by the Master of the vessel. Before I left the bridge, I spoke to the on duty and on site security vessel. He said that all was quiet and that I should have a nice evening. He told me that we would be the only vessel at the Idoho safe anchorage that night. The Idoho platform was 1.5 nautical miles away, and the security vessel was in between us both. The security vessel did not drop anchor but would normally drift about the sea and keep an eye on the platform and vessels in the area.

I then headed to my cabin to try to get a few hours' sleep. As usual, I went to bed in a T-shirt and boxer shorts and even with the air conditioning on it was still too warm for anything more than a thin sheet. The gentle lapping of the water outside and the whirr of the diesel generator were all I heard as I dropped off.

# 2

## PIRATES COME IN THE NIGHT

*Boom! Boom! Clang! Clang! Boom! Boom! Clang! Clang!*

I was jolted out of my dreams by loud banging and crashing, and the sound of metal pounding on metal. Beyond my cabin, there were also loud noises of smashing glass and breaking metal, coming directly from the bridge and adjoining passageways. I was rudely awakened from my sleep and wondered what the hell was happening. Why was there glass being broken? Why were there unfamiliar voices shouting and screaming? All of a sudden things got a lot worse, the generator stopped and the emergency lights came on, and at this stage I did not know what to think or do. There seemed to be many unfamiliar voices, talking in pidgin English and local languages that I did not understand.

The violent crashing sounds were getting nearer and nearer, and I could now hear lots of shouting. As the banging and crashing became louder I realised that we were being attacked and that our assailants were smashing down the iron security gate between the bridge and the accommodation. For a moment I was disoriented, until I remembered I was in my cabin with its small bed, side table and bedside cabinet. I also had some wardrobes, book shelves with a selection of books and well-thumbed sea-faring manuals. There were also a few lockers, a mirror and a chair beside my office desk. There

13

were two doors: one to the passageway and the other to a very small en suite toilet with shower. I was barefoot wearing only boxer shorts and a T-shirt as I slid out from under my cover. As I stood listening to the shouting getting louder, more high pitched, more aggravated and extremely excited, I struggled to fathom what exactly was happening and what my next move should be. Could I escape into the passageway and make a run for it? Or maybe I would stand more of a chance if I stayed where I was. All sorts of thoughts were racing through my mind, and not for the last time, I was petrified beyond belief. I had experienced scary moments before in Nigeria, but this was a different kind of fear. There is being scared and there is being petrified, in this instance I was petrified.

I glanced at my watch. It was almost 1am. It was still dark outside. My mind raced and heart pumped. I was shaking with fear now, I did not know what to expect. I knew of other vessels that had been attacked in Nigeria and expats that had been killed, so at this stage I feared the worst. I now realised that we were definitely being attacked and that my fate was in someone else's hands.

I locked my cabin door and thought that I should try to hide. My mind was racing – what was I going to do? I was very scared, I could not think straight, and panic was now gripping at my nerve ends. Was I going to die tonight? I had no wish to confront anyone with guns. This was something that was always stressed during our security drills – do not antagonise the attackers, do what you are told and give them what they want. Most importantly, do not show any aggression towards your attackers whatsoever. What should I do for the best? I kept thinking, if I am going to die tonight what will my wife Helen and the rest of my family do? These thoughts were continually going through my mind, yet still I had to focus on the here and now, and the imminent danger outside my cabin door. I thought, my God what do I do now?

As the shouting and screaming got closer, the more scared I became. The voices were raised and sounded so angry. I scrambled into the en suite toilet, locked the door and curled up behind the door close to the loo. It went quiet for a minute. At this point I was very scared. I thought the time had come and that the attackers were going to get me and kill me. I felt certain I would die, and I did not even contemplate the possibility of being held hostage for ransom money. It seems strange now but in that moment when I was terrified, it was difficult to think straight and consider any outcome other than death.

The en suite was very small and the space between the toilet bowl and the wall was tiny. I knew that I would not be safe in there. The flimsy walls and weak door were not going to protect me, but it was the only thing I could think of at the time – there was nowhere else to go.

*Bang! Bang! Bang! Craaack! Craaack!*

The crashing and banging sounded like a tree being split open and felled. It was ear-shatteringly loud and now much closer. I assumed that this was my cabin door being smashed open. I pushed myself as far into the corner of the toilet as I could. Now I was beyond petrified and shaking uncontrollably. There seemed to be lots of hammers banging repeatedly before the banging suddenly stopped. The assailants had now obviously gained access to my cabin. I wondered if my crew were safe. I had not heard gunshots, so maybe this was a good sign. Then I heard the unfamiliar voices again in my cabin. They were obviously smashing up the wardrobes, the bed drawers and the computer desk. Then there was a juddering crash on the toilet door, followed by five or six strikes on the door. All of a sudden I was faced with the head of a large sledgehammer. The sledgehammer made for a very dangerous weapon in the wrong hands. Fragments of the door were scattered over me, and as the door disintegrated I shouted out.

"OK, OK, OK, I'm coming out. Please stop hammering. I am opening the door," I pleaded.

I was scared that the sledgehammer was going to hit me on the head. I had never faced a situation like this before and was truly terrified. The sledgehammer was pulled from the splintered door as I unlocked it. I put my hands over my head. When the door was wrenched open I saw several tall men – probably half a dozen – pointing machine guns at me. Two of the men were tall and were dressed in dark clothing. Another two were of medium build and were dressed in combat style clothes, and the remaining two were smaller and were also wearing combat style clothing. Meanwhile, there were obviously other attackers going through the rest of the accommodation, as I could hear voices shouting and screaming in the other cabins.

"Don't shoot, don't shoot," I shouted.

I was grabbed by two attackers and hauled into my cabin which was now completely ransacked with pieces of furniture and glass all over the floor. My bedding was also scattered over the floor and my cabin was now unrecognisable. The attackers that grabbed me were dressed in green combat-style trousers and black vests. Most of the attackers were also wearing scarves tied around their neck and faces or dark balaclavas. At this point I could see very little or nothing of their faces. From their rough voices I knew that my attackers were Nigerian as I had heard a variety of local languages and pidgin English during my 11 years in Nigeria.

"You, Captain?" said one of the men in broken English, prodding me with his gun.

"Yes," I said and nodded.

Then he poked his machine-gun – I later learned it was an AK-47 Kalashnikov – close into my face.

"Where's the ship's money?"

I pointed to one of the lockers in the wardrobe, he indicated with the gun to open it.

"No tricks. No tricks," he warned.

Barefooted, I painfully walked through the debris scattered on the floor. I bent down and opened the safe, and gave them all the money we had on board. It was 37,000 Naira (£200) for the crew's expenses. They counted it up and started shouting at me. One of my deckhands earned 25,000 Naira per week, so 37,000 Naira was only slightly more than a week's wages for one ordinary working Nigerian – not a lot to share between a band of pirates.

"Where's the money? Where are the dollars? There must be a big sum of dollars. Tell us, Captain, or we shoot you now," they threatened. This was the first of many threats and the first time that someone had told me they were going to shoot me. I was scared beyond belief and trembling like nothing on earth.

"This is all there is," I said. "We don't keep dollars on the ship." I found it very difficult to speak

The two tallest attackers grabbed hold of me and told me that they did not believe me. I told them that I was too scared to lie. I explained that my company was Irish and that they did not allow us to have dollars on board and any of the crew could verify this. For a moment the cabin was silent. One of the pirates then violently ripped my two gold necklaces from my neck, while another snatched off my earring. Luckily the clasp opened and my ear was still in one piece,

One of the attackers forced me to take off my watch and my wedding ring. My shaking was uncontrollable and I was scared beyond belief. In a fit of rage one of the pirates proceeded to smash up the wardrobe and the safe with his large sledgehammer. After making sure they had everything of value from my cabin, one of the pirates said in a loud and angry voice, "Right, Captain. You are coming with us."

I felt like my world was crashing around me. All the jewellery that Helen had bought me over a period of some years had been ripped from my shaking body. It was not the cash value that I was thinking of but the sentimental value; Helen had given me the jewellery with love and these guys had ripped it from me with no feelings whatsoever.

I was then marched at gunpoint up to the bridge in my bare feet. They were saying to each other in pidgin English that we were heading for their small craft, and they were sure that they had ransacked everywhere and taken everything of any value. They told me to walk quickly and not to stop. With so many guns pointed at me I had no intention of stopping. All the ship's passageways and stairwells were littered with debris and my crew's personal effects. Empty wallets, ID cards and clothing lay everywhere, and every one of the cabin doors had been smashed beyond repair; we had spent a lot of time in the dry dock getting the vessel looking good, now it was unrecognisable. I was obviously primarily concerned for my safety and how this would all end, but seeing the *St Patrick* like this broke my heart. All the way up to the bridge, the stairs were strewn with broken glass from the bridge windows; this was not good for my poor bare feet. I could see the wheelhouse floor was also covered in broken glass from the smashed windows. I was very scared but tried to stay calm and not provoke my attackers in any way. All the way through the bridge was broken glass, shredding my bare feet. I was wondering where the two night duty watchmen were. Since we had left the cabin I had not seen any of my crew, and, except for the attackers, the bridge was empty of personnel. From the bridge I was taken down to the *St Patrick*'s main deck, where I could see two small open-boats alongside my vessel. These boats were about 8 metres in length, each with powerful outboard engines. There were more pirates, some with AK47s, and others with machetes and pump-action shotguns. Most of these guys were tall, wearing combat-style clothing with their faces covered. It was very dark and I could see little apart from the faint lights from the shore and the lights from the vessels scattered in the distance

When the pirates in the boats saw me they were shouting and gesticulating between themselves, it was as if they were arguing with each other. My senses were jangling and I felt in grave danger. I had to do everything I was told so as not to antagonise the highly-charged attackers.

"Get in the boat now!" one of the leaders shouted, pointing at the vessel alongside.

I did not want to leave the *St Patrick* and my crew but this wasn't the time to do anything brave or stupid. I certainly did not want to get hurt or even worse, shot. I thought about jumping into the water, but did not think I would be able to swim because of the trembling that had overcome me. The attackers would most likely shoot me in the water anyway, so I decided to continue to do what I was told and hope a solution would present itself later.

"Please, take what you want. But I need to stay on my ship, I am the Captain" I blurted out.

"Get in the boat now – or we kill you," said one of the pirates.

This was no time to be heroic. I made my way from the deck to one of my own vessel's rubber fenders, and stepped gingerly into the fibre-glass boat, which was lapping up and down on a light swell. Bizarrely, there was still no sign of any of my crew. What had happened to them all? Surely they had not just disappeared. Had some of them escaped, I wondered. When I was on board the small boat, another large attacker wearing a face mask poked his machine-gun right in my face. His English was not very good but understandable. "Sit down and be quiet," he growled. This guy seemed to be very young and quite angry and abrupt in the way he spoke to me. It appeared that he had been involved in some sort of accident as he was putting all his weight on his right leg and was leaning over to one side. All Nigerians have different tribal marks on their faces, this marking is normally done by their parents shortly after birth. The reason for this, according to Nigerians, is so they can tell each tribe apart. These marks are normally done with hot knives and are quite deep. Some will have one line and some will have two lines and so on. Even a lot of the women have these tribal marks.

Although it certainly wasn't cold, I was shivering with fear and was cowered down in the boat. I sat there in silence, shaking, as this noisy and extremely volatile gang continued to ransack my vessel. With their guns strapped over their shoulders, they formed a chain handing down various items from my vessel. There was a laptop, and an iPad, a television, two mobile phones, and an iPad and some other small items which I recognised from my cabin. I saw the large 50-inch television and the stereo unit from the officers' lounge coming down. I also saw several mobile phones, which I recognised as belonging to my crew. I thought of the hard-earned money they had put into their mobile phones and thought it was a crying shame. Some of the pirates were waving the mobile phones about as trophies and boasting about what they had done. All the time this was going on there were two guards pointing their guns at me to make sure I went nowhere.

There was loads of food coming down from the three food stores: tins of ham, corned beef, beans, carnation milk, bread and bread rolls, which my camp boss had baked that day, and cases of bottled water and various juices.

At this point I still hadn't seen any of my crew. I later learned from Chris that the attackers grabbed eight of my crew and beat up four of the guys who tried to resist the attackers. The chief officer told Chris that the lads that were beaten up were hit with the butts of the attackers' rifles. They ended up with bruised faces and black eyes. They were then released and told to say nothing. The rest of the crew hid in tanks to avoid the attackers and waited until about 5am before calling Exxon Mobil, the onshore marine coordinator and Chris. They were terrified to show their faces too early and wanted to make sure the attackers had all left the vessel. Chris explained that the watch keepers tried to run when the pirates started smashing the bridge windows: one managed to escape and hide but was caught and beaten by the attackers. He was forced to show the pirates where they wanted to go. The cabins were a target, especially my cabin and Victor's – the chief engineer. When the attackers grabbed Victor he tried to steer them away from my cabin but the pirates forced him to do otherwise. They also managed to get a hold of Nde, forcing him to open the food store. The store was always locked at night and the pirates made Nde help them carry the food and water up to the deck. Both Victor and Nde were bashed about by the pirates and received bruises for their efforts. Most of the crew managed to avoid the pirates, but the ones the pirates did get their hands on were terrified, as they knew what their own kind could do.

Afterwards I learned that Victor and Nde had begged with the pirates not to take their captain, but these pleas fell on deaf ears.

There are not a lot of hiding places on the St Patrick but the crew knew the vessel better than the pirates and managed to conceal themselves in hidden nooks and crannies. It was pointless for the pirates to kidnap another Nigerian – there was no money in that. They were only interested in 'rich' expats, and, luckily for them but unluckily for me, I was the only one on board that night.

As I sat trembling low in the boat, the attackers were loading their contraband. I was shaking with fear but I could not do anything to help myself, or anything to stop the pirates doing what they were doing. A few metres away the other motor boat was now circling the St Patrick. The bow of the boat I was in was now laden with all the booty scavenged off the St Patrick, and the pirates began leaping back into the small craft. It bounced and joggled in the water as each member landed on board. Every time one of them jumped on board the small boat gave a lurch and I was tossed about. There was still loud shouting and arguments going on. It was obvious that the pirates were not happy with the amount of cold hard cash they had plundered from my vessel. The pirates were shouting in Pidgin English, "The money is no good!" "The money is nothing!" Moments later the engine revved and we sped off into the dark night, skirting the tops of the waves and bouncing about everywhere. I could not help but contemplate what was going to happen next. Never in my worst nightmare did I think that I would ever be in a situation like this, and although I had a certain amount of training in vessels being attacked, nothing had prepared me for what was happening now. Outside of the training room, knowing what to do in this situation was impossible. In my mind I just had to go along with these guys, take things as they come and try to manage as best I could. At this point I thought the attackers would be taking me to some sort of hideout, but I heard the pirates saying that the money they received from my vessel was no good and if that was all they could get, their night had been a waste of time. Some of the pirates said, "But we have a captain." Whilst another replied, "It is still not enough for our night's work and we needed more cash!" I heard one of the pirates say that there were other larger vessels in the area and that they should attack another. I even heard one of the pirates say that they should attack another vessel and take the vessel as a hiding place for me, but the two guys who seemed to be in charge disagreed with this idea. They said they would attack another vessel to get some more cash and then take me to the jungle.

On board the ship I had a chance but what was going to happen now? I was a captive in a hostile craft in a vast expanse of water in the middle of the night. I felt the salty spray on my lips and gulped, but my throat was bone dry. I began to think I would never see my wife, my family and my home in Scotland ever again.

It was about ten minutes later that we approached another vessel. It was a massive oil tanker, it was a large black hulled vessel with a white superstructure, and she was probably about 130 metres in length, towering high above our craft with a very high wheelhouse. I was ordered to stay in the bottom of the boat and keep quiet. The pirates were shouting, some were pointing at the tanker and others were shaking their heads. We reached the tanker, and by now I was drenched by the sea spray. I was chilled and wet through, with goose bumps on my skin. I was intensely scared. If there were armed security guards on board the tanker, there could be an exchange of gunfire, and any shots aimed at the pirates' small boats could spell disaster for me. There was no protection for me sitting here and I could be killed or wounded in the crossfire. The terrifying thing was, I could do nothing to help myself. I thought about trying to jump in the water when most of the pirates were going to be on the tanker. But what would I do once I was in the water? The pirates would be sure to catch me and maybe shoot me out of sheer anger and frustration. I decided to stay put and take my chances with the pirates.

The tanker was at anchor with very few lights on. We pulled along the portside while the other motorboat disappeared to the starboard side. The pirates threw up ropes with grappling hooks to latch onto the vessel's railings. One of the younger guys was remarkably agile at shimmying up the rope. He passed other ropes down the vessel's side to make it easier for the pirates to gain access. There was plenty of shouting as they tried to bludgeon their way into the vessel. They left about 3 pirates on each motor boat and the rest boarded the tanker. I sat still, squinting up at the scene that was unfolding above. For perhaps 20 minutes they battered the steel doors into the wheel house and accommodation, and any hatches they could find, but made no headway. I imagined all the doors and hatches into the vessel were barred and double plated with steel, and their sledge hammers could not penetrate the stronghold. The only windows were high up on a wheel house, perched way up on the superstructure. There were no ladders, so the pirates could not reach it and gave up. The crew were perhaps aware that the pirates were on board their ship but they had the sense not to show their faces. They were a lot safer inside. The pirates went round the whole ship trying to gain entry but she was locked up everywhere and obviously there was no way in. Basically she was a fortress. I imagined that the company had the vessel prepared for attacks and the crew were well versed on what to do in the event of a pirate attack.

The pirates jumped back on board the small boats, stamping with fury at their fruitless attack. I slunk back further in the bottom of the boat. I was worried that they would direct their anger and frustration towards me. This was all a hellish nightmare. Where and how would it end? I was certain it would end in some violent confrontation. Increasingly, I feared I would not survive.

As the boats sped off again, the pirates were talking in a form of pidgin English, which I could understand. If they had been speaking in their native languages I would not have understood what they were saying. They wanted to carry on their sea assaults. As they had no joy with the previous vessel it was clear they were heading for another tanker, determined to get something out of their night's work. Perhaps there would be armed guards on this vessel? Would gunfire break out this time and would I be killed in the crossfire? The journey between the two vessels seemed to take forever, it was still darkish, and there were stars glinting in the sky, and Mr Moon was glowing brightly. All through the passage between the vessels the pirates talked and shouted at each other about what they were going to do next. Every now and again the lad with the bad leg would tell me to stay still and be quiet, and if I did what I was told I would be alright.

I was shivering with pins and needles in my wet arms and legs, but this was not my concern. My fear was for my life. Ten minutes later we reached the next vessel. I was unable to make out the name of the vessel in the dark but I learned later that it was called the *Lady Swathin*. Using the same tactics, the pirates all climbed on board leaving two guards to keep an eye on me. They could not believe their luck, there was a stairwell up to the back of the wheelhouse and the door was unlocked. The guards gave me the same order – 'do not move, stay quiet and stay still'.

"Stop. Don't move or we shoot!" shouted a pirate from the deck high above. There was obviously crew in the bridge. I felt vulnerable lying in the bottom of the boat awaiting the return of the kidnappers. It didn't take long. Soon the boats were being loaded again, this time with valuables taken from the tanker, there were 5 or 6 laptops, televisions, umpteen mobile phones, iPads, iPods and other electronics. There was more food being passed down as well, such as tins of biscuits, bottled water, cans of meat and cases of long-life milk. They did not take any of the personnel, so obviously there were no expats on board. The pirates were laughing and joking, now happy with their night's haul. I heard one of the pirates ask another one, "How much money did we get?" The answer was, "Over a million Naira." (£4,300). "So at least now we have some money for expenses," I heard another pirate say.

By now all the pirates had returned to the two small craft, and the boats seemed to be overloaded with items stolen from the two vessels and personnel. There was no space to move, I was curled up in a ball, shaking with fear and still wondering what my fate was going to be. We started to speed away from the tanker. It was two motorboats racing recklessly to the shore.

"Keep moving faster. It's not long till daylight!" yelled one the pirates, as a younger man pulled down the throttle of the outboard engine.

We were now zipping across the dark water at a fair lick towards the lights and the settlements on the Nigerian coastline. It was then that they turned their attention towards me. All, except the driver, began to stare at me intently. Then a young man – not much older than 14 – grinned at me. I could see his brown, discoloured teeth and the white eyeballs of a fresh-faced boy, with some stubble on his chin and upper lip.

"OK, Captain. You are coming with us now. We hope your company has plenty of money. We want 200 million Naira (£800,000) for you. If your company not pay, we set you on fire and burn you alive." I told him that my company was a small company and that I did not think they had that amount of cash. He said, "You better hope they can get it." I begged him not to do such a thing and that my boss Chris Woolley would do everything in his power to find the money.

This was truly terrifying. It was a threat that was so matter of fact, so nonchalant, so cold, yet I knew that it was real. I have been led to believe that being burnt alive would be the worst ever death. So to be told by someone that he was going to set me on fire was my worst nightmare. This young lad seemed to have no respect for others and would do what he could to get what he wanted. As a seaman I have always feared being drowned, but I have attended several firefighting courses and the horror stories that some of the instructors have told us about people being burnt alive is beyond belief. That threat will stay with me forever.

Daylight was now starting to creep over the sky as we approached the shore at full speed. The sea spray was covering us all, turning us white with the specks of salt. But I didn't care, I was still too stunned by what the young pirate had said to me. The land was clearly in view now and the kidnappers kept looking back over their shoulders to make sure they were not being followed. The coast was clear for them. I could now make out several entrances to tiny creeks concealed by dense jungle foliage that ran down to the shore. I shivered at the prospect of going ashore. I knew it would be impossible for anyone to find me if we ended up in one of the hidden mangrove creeks that fed into this expansive river estuary. The jungle creeks are situated amongst very dense jungle, there are no roads and the jungle can only be penetrated by small boats. Once we were in the jungle it would be impossible for anyone to find me. This bunch of pirates would make sure of that. I prayed that one of the Exxon Mobil security vessels was going to come and rescue me at the last minute, just before we arrived at the creeks. In reality I knew that this was not going to happen, but in my situation, I had to at least hope.

Where was I going? Where were they taking me? It was almost daylight and I could see some wooden huts with palm roofs, and a few smaller fishing boats bobbing at their moorings. The pirates were becoming increasingly agitated, they urged the driver to speed up and get to their camp as quickly as possible. Their mission was ending whilst my ordeal was just beginning.

# 3

## OFF TO OBLIVION IN A JUNGLE CLEARANCE AND MY FIRST DAYS IN CAPTIVITY

Our motorboat turned at high speed into the entrance of one of the hidden creeks which was obscured by creepers and raffia palms. We emerged into a wider lagoon and for a while headed towards another narrow creek where the murky water was calmer. I knew we had come out of the sea at the entrance to the Calabar River with its tree-lined islands but I was completely lost after that. Calabar is a very large village not far from the Cameroon border, and is one of the last points of major population in Nigeria just before Cameroon.

We seemed to go on forever, weaving round bends and through swamplands that were sometimes so narrow the boats had to slow down. In some of the creeks the water was very shallow and one of the pirates on the bow tested the depth of the water with a long stick. Each creek became narrower with the creepers tangling down and touching our boat. The swamp vegetation was lush and green and there were all sorts of exotic diving birds, shrieking and chirping, and insects buzzing and dipping in and out of on the water.

As the warmth of the day began, I was beginning to lose all hope of ever being found. I was already exhausted by the shock of my situation. The Nigerian navy vessels or Exxon security vessels would never be able to find me in these creeks. I was sure of that. Even if they did try to search for me, it would be an impossible task. I thought to myself, these guys know what they are doing. They could hide me in here for years or they could kill me. When captured, most of the hostages in Nigeria are taken to cities. This was very unusual. I doubted whether anyone, even local guys, could find their way through this jungle labyrinth. I kept hoping that we were being followed but these pirates were simply too careful. We went up a lot more creeks than necessary, just to make sure that nobody or no vessel could get to us. Even a spotter plane or a helicopter would be unable to make out the channels and creeks from above.

Everyone in the boat was now very quiet. There was little conversation between the pirates. My mouth was bone dry and I asked for a drink of water. I got no reply. The guys never even gave me a glance, they just seemed to ignore my request. The humidity was becoming more intense as the sun climbed in the sky. A pirate was puffing on one of my St Moritz taken from my cabin, and the wonderful aroma of tobacco wafted over me. I plucked up the courage and gestured with my two fingers to my mouth. To my surprise, the guy lit one and handed it to me. That first gasp of menthol in my throat and the exhaling of the smoke out through my nose was a single moment of ecstasy. I was still alive. I savoured the rest of the cigarette feeling the filtered tip on my salty lips. This helped calm me down. Now, I know that cigarettes are not good for you but because I was a smoker then, a cigarette seemed like a good thing at the time, basically because I had nothing else.

We motored up one of the narrowest creeks yet, and suddenly turned to port – or to the left in layman's terms. There was a tiny opening underneath a canopy of tall palm trees. We entered this opening very carefully as there were overhanging trees and thick bushes and headed towards a very steep bank. The second boat overtook us with great care and entered the very narrow channel. We then followed it onto the steep bank.

The boats stopped, the crews jumped out gingerly, and scaled the banks, slipping at times on the muddy embankment. The pirates immediately began offloading their haul for the night, handing it up to their mates at the top of the bank – cases of water, tinned food, and tinned and fresh milk. Of course there was also the more important stuff such as televisions, laptops, iPads, iPods, mobile phones and radios. I recognised a lot from my vessel, but there was also a lot of stuff I did not recognise. This must have obviously come from the tanker. When they finished clearing the boats, the remaining pirates hauled the boat I was in out onto the lower part of the bank. Once our boat was secured to the other boat a pirate handed me a pair of socks and a pair of tracksuit bottoms. They were actually my own items of clothing that the pirates had taken from my cabin. Did this mean that they actually cared? Could people who cared now, actually kill me later? I tried hard to figure out what these pirates were thinking. Perhaps they were just going to make sure I remained alive until they got their money. I was certain the money was the most important thing to them, and who knew what they would do with me after they had gotten what they wanted? Only time would tell.

I quickly wriggled the pants and socks on. At that point the socks were a godsend as I did not fancy walking up the muddy bank in my bare feet, and what lay beyond the steep bank was anyone's guess. The guys on the bank cleared a passage in order to get me up the steeper part of the bank. This took time as it was now strewn with everything they had stolen from the two vessels.

"Stand up, Captain. Time to get out," shouted one of the pirates, brandishing his gun.

I stood up falteringly in the bow of the boat as it rocked, then two pirates on the bank stretched out and pulled me up, while two in the boat pushed me from behind. I slithered and slid up to the top of the bank where I could now see a man-made clearing with several freshly-chopped tree stumps where more men had gathered. I could also see a small makeshift hut. I could hardly move for TVs, electrical goods and other supplies they had plundered. The trees had recently been cut down and the branches used to build the hut. The clearing was surrounded by tall, dense palm trees on every side and you could only see the sky directly above the clearing. The clearing was not big at all, and had been kept to a minimum to prevent it from being spotted from the air. The floor of the clearing was covered in sharp spikes. This was obviously where trees had been chopped down to make two small apartment huts. I wondered how longthis badly cleared spot of jungle was going to be my home. I could never have imagined living in a place like this. How could these guys live here? Most people wouldn't put their pets in a place like this, let alone a human being.

There were some long strands of rope and string hanging from the upper branches. I didn't know what this was all about and I shivered. I would find out the purpose of these ropes later.

This was an extremely remote place in the midst of an untamed, tropical jungle. It was an ideal hideout and it was unlikely that anyone, other than the gang and their allies, could ever find this hellhole. They were safe here while the hostage negotiations began.

When we congregated in the jungle clearing I saw the uncovered faces of most of the gang for the first time. The gang consisted of around 20 pirates, every one of them armed with either AK47s or pump-action shotguns. Some were small and of slender build, some of medium height and build, but most of them were tall and well built. Based on the size of their biceps, it looked like most of them went to the gym and did weight lifting. Regardless of age, many Nigerian men are completely bald with shiny heads. These pirates were no different.

I was escorted at gunpoint to the hut by the 14-year-old lad that had told me he was going to set me on fire. He too had no hair and a shiny bald head. Although he was slim and diminutive in stature he still had plenty of muscles, so had obviously done his fair share of training as well. I was told in a rough childlike voice to enter inside the hut. This hut was to be my home for I did not know how long. It was very basic, my half seemed to be a lot smaller than the other half, which was clearly for the pirates. At this point there was nothing in the pirates half of the hut, so they were obviously just about to set everything up, which made me think that this hut and the clearance had been purpose-built for my kidnapping. My side of the hut had a wooden bed and that was it. The walls and roof were made from pine tree branches and spikes woven together with small and large ants crawling everywhere. The makeshift hut was split into two compartments. My part was cramped and tight with four upright wooden posts with four rough wooden spars across the post. It was crawling with flies and insects. There was no room to stand up straight and I was hunched on the floor. Three more rough wooden planks were laid over the spars. This was my bed for the remainder of my stay. There were several gaps between the walls which allowed me to see some of what was going on in the clearing. The other larger section was for the pirates, and had a more solid wooden frame with sharp pine needle branches. A constant stream of marching ants – hundreds upon hundreds – were crawling over the earthen floor, onto the planks of wood and then up the wall. As soon as I lay down on the planks, the small ants began crawling all over me. The hut was also infested with flies and mosquitoes that kept landing on my naked arms, legs and face. I was getting badly bitten. I tried to swat them away but there were far too many. Very soon I had bad sores and red lumps all over my skin. I was itching like mad, and the tiny beasts just kept on biting. After some time, two of the gang came into the hut, and introduced themselves as Nick and Thomas, although I did not believe for one minute that these were their real names. They had the bearing of gang leaders and it looked like they were both in their late 20s or early 30s. They were both tall, probably over six feet, and muscular. Nick had a bald head and a well-trimmed beard, while Thomas wore a red and yellow baseball cap that belonged to me. The annoying thing was that they were both dressed in my tracksuit bottoms and T-shirts. They both carried machine guns around their necks and shoulders which had high-strength duct tape wrapped around the handles and magazines. The other gang members were of various ages and sizes, but even the youngest guys had bald shiny heads. The younger guys even looked prematurely aged because of their lifestyles and the sun in Nigeria.

Most of the pirates were in their bare feet and dressed in clothes stolen from the vessels they had attacked that night. Nick and Thomas, however, had on my footwear. Thomas was wearing my dress shoes for travelling and Nick had my trainers on, which looked too big but this didn't seem to bother him. Thomas and Nick angrily told me in broken English that I had to behave and stay in the hut. An older chap came in to the hut, he was called 'Elder Brother', and even Nick and Thomas seemed to look up to him with a sense of respect. He seemed to be in his mid-forties, with the same bald and shiny head, but he was quite plump compared to the rest of the pirates which made me think he was superior in rank to the others. He also spoke reasonably good English and seemed to be educated. The three of them then spoke in a native language which I could not understand. Once they had finished they told me not to cause any trouble and that I would be fine.

Nick then showed me my two mobile phones, one a Nokia and the other a new Galaxy S3 Mini.

"Are these your phones?" he asked in broken English.

"Yes, both are my phones," I replied. It was obvious that they had taken the phones from my cabin when they took me, so it seemed like they were well organised and that they had everything planned – they had obviously kept my phones separate from all the other phones they had stolen that night.

"We'll be contacting your boss tomorrow. If he agrees to our demand for 150 million Naira (£612,000), we will take you and go and meet him and we will transfer you for the money. Then you will be allowed home," said Nick in rough, broken English. At this stage I did not believe that I would ever get out of there, the money they were talking about was unrealistic and I knew that Chris did not have that sort of money at hand.

"Why are you not contacting him today?" I asked.

"Well, we have our reasons for not doing it until tomorrow. Don't worry, just behave and you will be fine. You tell us if there is anything you want."

I did not believe at that point that I was going to be fine. I thought this was just talk and they were only saying these things until they received their money.

"I want some food and water, please."

"We can't get you food today but we can give you some bottled water for now and you will get more tomorrow." Again I found it difficult to accept what he was telling me as the truth. Something in the way he was barking at me in broken English told me not to trust him. They were pirates after all, could I believe anything they were telling me? I knew they had taken plenty of bottled water from the two vessels, so why were they telling me I would get more tomorrow and only give me a small ration for now, it seemed to me that they were making sure there was plenty of water for themselves for the foreseeable future. My mind was racing as I tried to get inside their heads. I tried to see just how hard these guys were in that short space of time. I wanted to see if at some point any of these two guys had any give in them, could I turn to either of the two for assistance as time passed? First impressions told me that Thomas was possibly a bit more giving than Nick. Nick seemed to be very hard in manner and gave me the impression that he would be very unforgiving.

They both walked out of my side of the hut into the clearance. Nobody was going to stay too long in my side of the hut as it was very small and very hot.

Much of the gang were chattering in their native tongue which I did not understand, whilst some of them conversed in pidgin English, which I could interpret. As the morning grew hotter, I heard more motor boats coming and going. People were now arriving who had had nothing to do with the actual attack on the vessels. There seemed to be quite a few people arriving. This made me feel even more uncomfortable as it meant that there would be even more sets of eyes watching my every move. Perhaps they had come from a local village and this was some kind of community event. I suspected that their entire village must have known about the vessels and the kidnapping. How could all these people armed with dangerous weapons come and go from villages without everyone knowing what they were up to?

Two of the pirates, dressed like armed guards, stood at each side of the clearing at all times watching the various activities. There were a couple of scythes and machetes lying around that had obviously been used by the pirates to clear the ground for walkways. One of the pirates tried to convince me one day that this was where they lived. He said because of the government there was no work in his part of Nigeria and that they had no money for houses and were being forced to live here like animals. He also said that if he did not work he did not receive any money, and what they were doing now was their only way to get money, and this was the kind of place they had to live in. I knew not to argue with him and just listened, nodding my head now and again.

As time passed I tried my best to get to grips with all of the pirates' behaviours and manners. I was looking for any sign of weakness in any of my captors that may have helped me in the days which were to follow. How could I use any of these guys to keep me safe? These thoughts were to occupy my mind until I was out of there, God willing.

There were a few buckets scattered around the clearing, like the ones you would wash your floor with. Some pirates used these for bathing, whilst others used them for their dishes, and they were piled high with bottles, plates and cups until someone would wash them when they needed them again. When the gang was bathing in the buckets, they would stroll around naked and it did not bother them in the slightest. There were a couple of small gas stoves out in the clearance where the pirates did their cooking. The small tree stumps that had been left after the trees had been felled were spread around the clearing and these were used as tables and seats by the pirates. They had a couple of flat pieces of Formica that they used on top of the tree stumps as table tops for playing cards, during my stay there the gang played cards day and night with wads of Naira. I couldn't see what game they were playing, but it obviously involved gambling and looked like some sort of poker. Sometimes a row would erupt and the arguments would get quite heated, with some pushing and shoving. When they were playing cards I always had my two guards with me. Sometimes another two guys would relieve them, so they could take part in the card games as well. I was very concerned when they started arguing that they may turn their anger towards me. I never took my eyes off them when they were arguing, as I was constantly worried that they might turn on me. The only thing that would stop them turning on me, I thought, would be the money. The whole gang was fuelled by drinking beer and local firewater and smoking the local ganja, a sweet-smelling weed which filled the air with its aroma. The beer was normal Nigerian beer, which was very potent, and the home made hooch was made in local villages. Each village has its own recipe, and the hooch was some sort of pure sprit, clear in colour with a strong smell. The ganja was also made locally, they grew the weed plants themselves but then added some sort of other plant to thin the

36

weed down, making it go further. I'd heard previously from some of my crew that the ganja was dangerous stuff. It was deeply worrying when they started arguing among themselves as they were all high. I was praying that they would not take their anger out on me. Most of the pirates were surprisingly well dressed in shorts and T-shirts. Some of the pirates were now wearing my clothes, taken from my cabin, I also recognised some of my crew's clothing, including their English Premier League football shirts. I tried to work out if there were any of these guys that may have a little sympathy for my plight. I tried to be positive and continued to hope that theses pirates had just taken me for the money and would release me when this was all over. I knew of cases where expats had been released after being kidnapped; however, I also knew of cases where the hostages had been killed. It was difficult to try to read the minds of the pirates here in this hideout. Remembering the advice from my Ships' Security Officers' course – never make the attackers angry, always make sure you don't antagonise them at any time – I tried to be nice at all times, so as not to make these guys angry.

Many of the gang ignored me and I sensed their contempt as they went about their business. Some would come and ask how I was but said no more. However, a younger pirate called Louey, who was often one of my guards, seemed talkative. One day when he was guarding me he decided to have a heart to heart, and asked me how long I had been in Nigeria and he even asked if I liked Nigerians. I told him that I had been in Nigeria for eleven years and that of course I liked Nigerians, and that most of my crew were Nigerians. I asked him why his group were carrying out kidnappings, and he said that they did it solely for the money, and that if they did not do these types of things his family would starve. I asked him if it was not too dangerous, especially for a lad his age.

Whilst cradling his machine-gun as if it were a baby, he told me he feared nobody.

"If anyone argues with me while I have my gun in my hand, I would have no hesitation in killing them," said Louey in good English.

This was scary, especially when he was the one guarding me. I tried to converse with him as best I could, whilst trying not to make him angry. Louey told me he had had a very hard upbringing and that his family was very poor and they had no house. He said they used to steal from the land just so they could eat. He was very bitter towards the Nigerian government.

"The government are taking lots of money from the oil fields in Nigeria but give the people of Nigeria nothing in return," he told me.

"If a Nigerian does not work or if they are sick, they are on their own and there is no help for them. If adults or children are sick and have no money, they are even turned away at the hospitals. With no money, there is no treatment," he continued. Louey told me that he had nothing against me personally but that he and his group needed the money that they stood to get for me. He clicked his gun's safety catch off and on. This made me a bit nervous, Louey complained that he had no money for medical care for his parents, and that this was another reason for his actions. I asked him if he did this sort of thing often but he refused to answer the question and looked a little angry. I regretted asking this question as it seemed to end the conversation. He stood up and went to the entrance of the small hut to smoke weed. It shocked me that someone so young would be smoking dope. I could not help feeling a little sorry for Louey, and what he was forced to do to survive. In Britain, if you are unemployed you get help from the government through unemployment benefit, income support etc. Louey told me that in Nigeria there is no help whatsoever for the unemployed or the sick. Thousands of people in Nigeria do not even have homes; instead, if they are lucky, they sleep in tin shacks. I feel sure that if the Nigerian government gave some of the revenue from the oil back to the people, there would be fewer pirate attacks. Kidnapping is a way of surviving for a lot of Nigerians.

I was wondering if perhaps the pirates had left a tell-tale trail that might lead wouldbe rescuers to this clearing. Surely someone was asking where is the captain of the *Saint Patrick* was? Most of the gang members like Louey were young and brimming with bravado and I wondered if they had been boasting in the villages about what they had done. I hoped that maybe someone with a conscious would report this incident to the authorities.

## 4

# HELL IN THE HUT

The pirates were wearing my jewellery that I had been given from my dear wife Helen. Thomas had on my gold Masonic pendant and gold chain, while Nick had my gold ship's wheel pendant with the thick gold chain round his neck. I saw another showing off my gold wedding ring, and another had my earring in his pierced ear. Seeing strange men wearing my belongings was something I had never in my life envisaged, and all this made me feel even worse.

They had taken my iPod too and were playing my favourite music –American country and western. It was so bizarre, I didn't know whether to laugh or cry when the songs of Dolly Parton burst out in the clearing. Passports and identity cards belonging to my crew were strewn across the ground, which made me think again if they were safe and unharmed. The crew's welfare was never out of my thoughts, and there were things that were happening that brought my crew to my mind more and more often. To see the photos of Victor the chief engineer, Benard the electrician and Nde the camp boss on the ID cards lying on the ground was very upsetting to say the least. Every time I went to the toilet or had to go to the trees with the phones hanging from them, I could see these pictures of some of my crew. I wondered what had happened to the rest of the ID cards; when the vessel was attacked every ID card for the crew on board was in my safe

40

in the cabin. So if they had some ID cards they had obviously taken them all. Every time I saw these pictures I became fearful for the crew's safety. I had no idea what had happened to them when I was snatched. Had they been killed? Were they still alive?

One day during my stay in the hut, I overheard the pirates in the clearing plotting another attack. They were going to hit the Mobil field again and attack two French supply vessels. They were oblivious to me listening but I could understand quite a bit as they were discussing their attack in pidgin English.

When the gang went to the toilet they disappeared deep into the jungle rather than down the steep banks. When I called to go to the toilet, they took me down a steep bank to the edge of the boggy swamp. At night, I hesitated with every step wondering if there were poisonous snakes and other dangerous animals hidden in the undergrowth. When I walked through the hut there were hundreds of ants of all sizes. Walking through this in my bare feet was not nice at all, and something that I had never done before. My skin was crawling. The ground outside the hut was littered with pine needles, again this was not nice to walk on. There were also empty food cans and containers thrown everywhere, which meant that just getting to the bog to go to the toilet was like going through an obstacle course. I had to slide down the bank in my bare feet to get to where I could go to the toilet, and thanks to severe diarrhoea I had to make this terrible journey on a regular basis. After doing the toilet, the two guys that had escorted me to the bog had to pull me back up the bank, where I then had to renegotiate the obstacle course and face the ants to get back to my cell.

During these long, tense hours and days in captivity, I thought continually about my family and friends back in Scotland. How were they coping with the news of my disappearance? I had been faced with dangerous situations before, but nothing like this – trapped in a jungle cage like an animal. How was Helen coping with this? I felt sure that she would have family and friends around her to help in her hour of need. I wondered if it would be better for her not to know, but if I was killed, God forbid, then she would obviously have to be told.

It was not only the exotic insects that I had never seen before that made my hut a living hell, but also the heat. I am not good in the heat at the best of times, and the temperatures that were being generated inside my small hut meant it was like being held captive in a furnace.

I was 15 years old when I was a deckhand on the Glenisla, and then my second vessel was the Netherley, both run by the North Star Fishing Group in Aberdeen. They were hardy vessels of about 20 metres long, built for fishing in the harsh Scottish waters, off the islands of Shetland and Orkney. I then joined the John Wood Group Company, owned by the man of the same name, which is now a massive global oil services group. Back then it was a company concerned with fishing trawlers in the North Sea and beyond. I was a deckhand on a large trawler sailing further out into the icy seas off the Faroe Islands and into the Arctic Circle off Iceland. I also went to college and passed my Third Hand certificate joining a vessel called the Red Crusader. The skipper was Teddy Wood, and was nicknamed 'Typhoon Ted' because he used to steam out and fish in terrible, stormy weather. Other more cautious skippers would head for port, but never Typhoon Ted.

One icy February we were working hard on the shifting deck off the Faroes in horrendous weather and deep waves. The shipping forecast was Storm Force Ten yet still we ploughed on. We were hauling our net and it was blowing a Hooley. The massive swirling waves were rolling down on us, when a sudden freak wave hit us right on the side of the vessel where we were working. The Red Crusader keeled heavily to starboard and then from nowhere another wave hit us and the vessel went even further over to starboard with the rail now under the water. I slipped and slid, trying desperately to hold on but I was washed over the side wearing my heavy boots and soaking oilskins. I threw up my hands in despair, yelling for help but I was swept over the side into the freezing ocean. For a split second I was filled with panic: I was far too young to die. All of a sudden a rough net grazed my hands and I grabbed hold. The Red Crusader rolled back to port spilling me and the net back onto the deck. I put my feet down I could not believe it when I felt the deck. It took a while for the seas to clear from the deck. The first thing we had to do was to check to see who was missing and to our surprise we were all still there. Another four of my shipmates had been washed overboard in the same way and they too had managed to grab the net. We were bruised and bashed but we had been saved. We knew someone or something was looking after us that day.

After the water cleared, the mate told us to stow the gear to make it safe and get off the deck. Typhoon Ted came thundering down onto the deck.

"What the hell are you all doing?" he yelled.

"We're putting the gear away, Skipper. It's far too rough," said the mate.

Ted shook his head and demanded we put the net back in the water again. We were all still shocked and dazed, and so we refused. We wanted to gather our senses, warm ourselves up and assess the damage. All the fish that were on the deck had been washed overboard so we had been risking our lives for nothing. Ted could see there was no point in arguing with us. After everything was secured on deck, we left the deck and headed for our accommodation. The passageways, accommodation, mess room and engine room were all flooded. We were lucky that the main engine and generators were still running. The skipper turned the engine to dead slow and headed the vessel into the wind. This was the best way to keep the vessel safe in the very big seas. After the storm passed, Ted wanted to continue fishing, but four of us refused and told him we wanted to go home. Ted was adamant that his vessel was not going home until it was filled with fish but he told us that he would put us ashore in the Faroe Islands and get replacement crew sent up. So we then headed for the Faroe Islands and left Typhoon Ted's trawler. After spending a few days stuck in Torshavn, the British consul helped us with some money and sent us home. The whole episode was a massive shock at the time, but we survived. I spent a few months ashore in Aberdeen wondering whether I would ever go back to sea. But the sea was already in my blood so I decided to return, but never again with Typhoon Ted.

I learned an important lesson. If I was going back to the fishing full-time, it would not be on an exposed deck hauling in the fish, it would be in the wheelhouse, looking after the vessel and the crew. That's where I wanted to be. I had to undertake a few more trips as a deckhand before I sat my Third Officer's certificate. The third officer is the person who is third in command of the vessel and is responsible for the fishing nets and other equipment. The skipper relies on him keeping the fishing gear in tip top condition – the better the condition the more fish you will catch. The third officer answers to the skipper and the mate of the vessel. During my shore leave, I refused to spend my time in Aberdeen's boozers knocking back whisky and vodka until oblivion, like far too many of my young colleagues. Instead, I worked hard at college and managed to pass the certificate first time. After another year of sea time as third officer on a couple of vessels I returned to college and sat my Mate's certificate.

I passed this and sailed as Mate on the *Admiral Nelson*, with a skipper called Ronnie Pirrie. The mate is second in command of the vessel, he is also in charge of the deck and all fishing operations on deck, and stowing the fish in the fish room. The better condition the fish are in when you land them the more money you will receive for them when auctioned at the fish market. Ron was a steely Icelandic fisherman who taught me a lot more about how to survive at sea. While he shared some of Typhoon Ted's traits in that he was unafraid to fish in some terrible weather, he was more tactical and always made an assessment about the risk and the reward. If there was likely to be enough of a catch, then this was worthwhile. He used to have us working in some very cold temperatures. Sometimes the Admiral Nelson was so cold it would ice up, which is dangerous for trawlers. Ronnie issued us with small axes for breaking the hanging ice off the ship's rails. On those long journeys to and from the Icelandic fishing grounds, Ronnie taught me how to play chess. I became proficient at the game and even started to beat Ronnie. After 18 months with Ronnie, I felt confident enough to sit for my Skipper's certificate, and passed it first time. The examiner congratulated me saying that this does not happen too often and many students have to re-sit their exams several times. I spent a couple of years as Skipper with the Wood Group sailing their deep sea trawlers, I then moved over to J Marr & Sons. This was like joining the Premier League. They were taking modern stern trawlers from the English ports of Hull and Grimsby. These were the vessels everybody wanted to be on as they were new, far more comfortable and better vessels in poor weather. Not only that, but the pay was good too!

These vessels had a crew of 12, most had a skipper, a mate, a third officer, a chief engineer, a second engineer, a cook and six deckhands. You learned how to get on with people. There were always times, because of the confined space and the long days at sea, when the crews did not see eye to eye. But you had to sink your differences, get over it and get on with the job in hand.

My back was stiff and sore now in this Nigerian hut as I tried to lie down on my wooden plank in the hut. If I did not have the accident on the platform I would probably still be working with

BP and I would not be in this predicament now. Life takes many twists and turns, you are never sure what is ahead. My mother always told me that when you are born your life is mapped out for you. Surely dying in this jungle wasn't my fate?

# 5

# LIFE WITH BP AFTER ABERDEEN TRAWLERS

My brother Roy worked for BP and said that I should take a more reliable job with a steady salary. He asked me to compile a CV, something I had never done before, and he handed it in to the personnel department at BP's head office in Dyce, in Aberdeen. I was taking a break, considering my next move, when I received a call from BP. They asked if I was available for a job interview as a deck operator. Sure, I was available and a date and time for an interview was arranged. It went extremely well. The personnel manager was impressed with my credentials, checked all my paperwork and explained what the job entailed. Two days later I received a call from BP saying I had been successful in my application. They wanted me offshore to join the Forties Bravo, a BP oil platform in the North Sea, as soon as possible. The Forties was one of the first great North Sea oil and gas fields discovered in 1970 and was about 100 miles north-east of Aberdeen. I was available at once, and they managed to get me booked on several safety courses. Roy was a production operator on the Forties Charlie, another platform in this field, at the time. It would have been ideal to work alongside him, but family members working offshore on the same rigs and platform was frowned upon. If anything disastrous happened, the remaining family would have had more to deal with than they could maybe handle. BP told me my salary and that I would be working on a rotation of two weeks on the platform and three weeks off. This all sounded great and Helen was delighted. Steady pay and more time at home. I had undertaken several courses already, so I only had to do the offshore survival, the helicopter evacuation and the banks man and slingers courses. I completed all three courses in two weeks and then went offshore where I joined my new workmates and made new friends. It was exhilarating being flown by helicopter from Dyce airport out over the North Sea. I smiled to myself as I watched the trawlers far below heading out to sea from Aberdeen harbour. I was introduced to everyone on the massive Forties manned platform, a monument of steel and piping, stairways, gantries and decking, that epitomised the booming oil industry. I met the operations manager, the supervisors, crane operators and catering crew. I did my induction where all safety procedures and emergency evacuations were discussed and I then received a tour of the platform. I was shown my muster station and my life boat station for drills and emergencies.

I was off duty in the evening, and sat down with my new colleagues for a getting-to-know-you-all chat. Jim Morrison, the deck foreman, shocked me when he told me about the platform's recent history. All the crew had been together for a long time. A few weeks earlier, six guys from one team had all been off duty and one of their colleagues, a man of about 34 years, did not turn up for breakfast before starting his shift. They checked to see where he was and found him lying dead in his bed. He had passed away in his sleep. I had been allocated the dead man's bed. This was an eerie experience for me and I could not stop thinking about the poor man's family.

I enjoyed my seven years with BP and encountered many interesting and decent folk. I completed more courses with BP, upping my pay grade, and continued to work on the Forties Bravo, sometimes doing relief work on the Forties Alpha,

Charlie and Delta platforms. But my time with BP came to a sad and abrupt end.

I was working in the pump room on the platform with two of my team and we were fitting two new sea water coolers. We were using a block and tackle to ease them into place. These were very heavy indeed, several tonnes in weight. We had to do the final positioning to get the bolts in with large bars called 'helpers'. I was on the bar and because there was not a lot of space I was crouched down putting all my strength behind the bar to get the bolt holes lined up. I was straining hard to keep things going when I felt something go in my back. There was a searing pain right through my back. After a few minutes it calmed down and felt a lot better. We went on to the second cooler. Again I threw my whole body strength behind the bar to line up the bolt holes. The next thing I knew I was in the BP platform sick bay. A concerned medic told me I had collapsed, blanked out and fallen quite a distance. I could not move my back and had severe pains down my left leg. The medic called the Aberdeen Royal Infirmary on the platform radio for assistance. He explained my symptoms to a doctor and the doctor advised that I should be given a morphine injection to alleviate the pain. The medic was also told that I should be kept under close observation for 24 hours and if things had not changed in that time the medic had to call them back. The next day my situation was worse and it was decided that I had to be flown ashore as soon as possible to Aberdeen Royal Infirmary. This was the last time I worked on a BP oil platform. The next two and a half years were torture. My back was in a terrible mess and I was in constant pain. There were many visits to the infirmary and referrals to many specialists. I was referred to a Canadian doctor, Mr Wardlaw, one of the top back specialists in the world. He had come over to the UK to assist surgeons in their understanding of back problems. I was on full sick pay from BP for over a year and then on half pay for the remainder of the time until I saw Mr Wardlaw. I was deeply frustrated, many doctors had told me that they could not identify the problem and that they did not want to operate on me. I spent long months lying on floors and in permanent pain. Mr Wardlaw examined me in ways that none of the doctors before him had done. He measured both legs and stuck pins all over my back and neck. If I agreed he would do an exploratory operation on me.

After the operation Mr Wardlaw came to see me and told me my back was a mess. I had a prolapsed disc which he removed, fusing the two discs above the prolapsed one together, so that they would not slip as well. This caused a problem for my work. Mr Wardlaw prepared a report for BP saying I would not be fit for any heavy duty in the future. When BP saw the report they called me into the office. Helen drove me to the office in Aberdeen and I hobbled in with the aid of walking sticks. The personnel manager said that because of the surgeon's report they had no other option but to medically discharge me. This was devastating news. BP were very fair and Helen and I would receive compensation, and a pension. Such is the roll of the dice in life.

# 6

# MY WORKING LIFE IN WEST AFRICA

So how did I end up in Nigeria?

After my accident on the BP platform and six months after my operation, I was kicking my heels with boredom. I was far too young to simply retire. I had to get back to work. Mr Wardlaw was clear: heavy duty work was not an option. However going back to sea as a ship's officer did not involve heavy lifting. I had a few friends that were sitting their 'dynamic positioning' certificates – DP was a new, increasingly popular thing for vessels in the oil industry. It made the positioning and operation of vessels a whole lot better and safer. So I returned to college and sat my DP certificate, paying for it myself, before I went back to sea.

My back was still painful and I had to take a cocktail of pain killers to keep me moving, but I felt worthwhile again. I've always been motivated by making a contribution to society. I applied for a vacancy with Svitzer Towing as Chief Officer and Junior DPO. Svitzer were a global company operating all over the world. I was successful and joined the Svitzer Magellan and, although it wasn't DP, I was Chief Officer for a couple of trips, then got promoted to Master. It was thrilling being back at sea on a working vessel that was ploughing through the North Seas. After a few months there was an opening for a Chief Officer on the Svitzer Mercator, which was a DP vessel. This was more appropriate for me as I would be using my DP certificate and skills. I was fortunate and after a couple of trips the Master resigned and I was promoted to Master – DPO. This held me in great stead for five years until I resigned and went to work for PW Resources.

PW Resources was then called Kent Base and a part of the PW Group, a reputable Irish engineering group and one of the largest in Nigeria. Its founder Hugo Flynn established PW Nigeria in 1974 just as the oil industry was taking off in the country. The company is well-known for its public works programmes, with housing, water, road and bridge building. In 1998, PW Resources was set up to serve the West African oil industry, and designed and built the *St Patrick* for this job. In January 2002, I prepared to fly out to join the *St Patrick* as joint Captain, working for Esso in Ghana, very close to the Nigerian Navy base in Sekondi.

My flights were booked and a visitor's visa was sent to me in Scotland giving me entry into Ghana. I flew to Accra, the capital, and I was met by the PW immigration officer. He took me to the airport immigration office and after about an hour and the handover of a substantial amount of local money, I received my working visa. We then drove to PW's offices in Accra. With PW Group being Irish-owned, most of the expat managers and staff working ashore were from all over Ireland. Brian, the base manager, welcomed me and informed me that I would be booked into the PW boot camp for the evening. The next day a driver would pick me up at 6am and take me to Sekondi, a four-hour drive away, where I would join the vessel. The staff house had three comfortable bedrooms, a kitchen and a lounge, and there was a cook. I met two other guys staying in the hostel who worked in the PW transport department. The cook, a Nigerian, made us some supper and then the guys suggested we head to the PW's bar in the camp. It was a pleasant evening as we walked down to the bar, next to an outdoor swimming pool where a few

PW workers, guests and a handful of locals were sitting around laughing and enjoying some drinks. I had a couple of beers, then went off to bed. I was impressed with the way PW looked after their people. At 5am I was up, washed and having breakfast, ready for the drive to the Sekondi naval base.

The driver picked me up at 6am on the dot, and I had my first real hard look at West Africa. It was a shocking eye opener. All along the roads, people were tucked up, sleeping on the sidewalks with no coverings at all. A few had a slither of corrugated iron roof for cover, and there were babies, children and adults bathing in insect-infested, stagnant pools of water. You could see a haze of mosquitoes everywhere. It was shocking to see such poverty at close quarters. I wondered what I had let myself in for. We passed several local markets selling piles of fruit, meat, fish and chicken. Again, there were flies everywhere. It was so unhygienic I could not believe what I was seeing. After half an hour, I asked the driver if we could stop so I could have a cigarette. He shook his head.

"We don't stop. Not safe. You can smoke in the car if you want, no problem," he said.

I pulled out a cigarette and lit up. I prefer not to smoke in the car but I was making an exception this morning. The day became warmer and the sun brighter. After about two and a half hours we arrived at a sprawling old colonial-style hotel right on the beach.

"We will stop here. You can get something to eat here. And there is a toilet," said the driver

It wasn't yet 9am but when I stepped out of the car the heat was ferocious, hotter than anything I had experienced in my life, even on holiday in Spain. I knew he had been given expenses for our food but he still got me to buy his breakfast. I wasn't too worried. He told me his salary was about £20 per a month, while I was on £250 a day, so I felt a bit guilty. The hotel was basic but we had a bite to eat before we continued our journey.

Just after 10.30am we arrived in the searing heat at the Sekondi naval base. We stopped at a checkpoint where two stern navy officers approached us. I showed my visa, my passport and Master's Certificate, giving them the name of the vessel.

"I'm the master of the *St Patrick*," I informed them proudly.

The gate officer instructed me to come to the office the next day to get a permanent naval gate pass that would allow me to go in and out of the base. The *St Patrick* was awaiting spare parts and would be there for another four to five days before we could continue with our contract with Esso Oil.

As we drove deeper into the dock area, there were a few ships of various types tied up, and there were some Nigerian Navy vessels waiting to sail on assignments. There were several large gantry cranes and some dilapidated warehouses in need of a paint. There were plenty of people milling around, although most were standing in the shade to keep the burning sun off their heads. Nearby was a fishing harbour where dozens of open-top boats were tied up with guys sitting grilling their fish on wrought-iron stoves whilst sipping beer.

The driver took me right to the quayside and we stopped at the *St Patrick*. It looked a sturdy vessel, with its massive crane and boom, the two-storey accommodation on the deck, and the wheelhouse overlooking the expansive deck area. There was a watch keeper on the gangway and he ushered me up the steps to the accommodation. A friendly and beaming Irish fella greeted me with a firm handshake.

"Hi Captain. Welcome to the *St Patrick*. I'm Tony," he said.

"Pleased to meet you, Tony. It's been an interesting journey. I'm delighted to be here."

"You'll be rather hot. Come and have some tea and a chat and then we can look around the *St Patrick* and meet your crew," he smiled.

Tony O'Neill was PW Resources' project manager for the Esso contract. Firstly I was shown to my cabin, a small room with its en-suite bathroom, where I dropped off my bags. Space was a premium on board and there were only three single cabins. The rest of the guys shared, some in two-man cabins and some in four-man cabins. The four-man cabins were very small but the personnel appeared to be happy enough.

After our tea, Tony took me on a tour and introduced me to the second captain, the chief officer, the second officer-DPO, the chief engineer, second engineer, dive supervisor and all the expat divers. They were all British or Irish guys and it would take me a bit of time to learn all of their names. I then met the deck and dive crew. Apart from the expat divers, there was a mixture of Ghanaian and Nigerian divers. In all, the crew totalled 40.

Next day, as I shifted through the paperwork, I discovered the vessel was registered in Nigeria and St Vincent and Grenadines, which was why we had to carry Nigerian crew members even when working in Ghana. We carried Ghanaians because we were working in their national waters. I pulled on my cap and headed back to the naval base office to get my pass. On the walk over I saw the 'bush' bars, several market stalls selling a range of local fruit and veg and some trinkets, and a few shops. In the naval office, I had my picture taken for my pass, I handed over my documents and the officer said it would take about an hour to process my pass. I decided to explore this bustling naval base and headed back towards the bush bars and shops. I ventured into one of the shops and was astonished to find every item was carved from ivory from elephants' tusks. It was an Aladdin's cave of different objects, some only a few pounds, others massively expensive. In all my years, I have never bought anything made of ivory, I knew about the ban on bringing it back to the UK, and how poaching is wiping out elephants.

That evening I got an interesting first impression of West Africans which marked my thinking for years to come. Some of the British guys invited me to join them in one of the bush bars. It was a pretty basic affair, with a fridge and a gantry of whisky and gin. There was a few rickety tables and chairs with the obligatory ashtray. We were joined by some of the Ghanaian and Nigerian crews. They never spent one penny and the expats picked up the tab for all the drinks. This kind of drinking culture would become a problem as time progressed.

# THOUGHTS OF MY WIFE HELEN HELP CALM MY FEARS IN THE HUT

The humidity inside the hut left me breathless, and there were flies and ants everywhere. During the first day in the hut, I complained to the pirates that I was too hot. They said that something would be done about the heat the next day. I was not allowed to leave the hut except for when I needed the toilet, and even then I had two armed escorts with me. I was parched and begged for water.

"Please, please give me some water!" I shouted

At first they ignored my calls and then after about two or three hours I was given four small plastic bottles of water.

"Make these last. We'll get you more tomorrow," said the guard handing me the bottles.

Yet I could see the pirates were splashing large bottles of water from the *St Patrick* into a basin that they were using for bathing. I was never given any food and I was desperate for another cigarette. I spied a couple of the guards puffing cigarettes although most of them were smoking a local form of dope.

"Please can I have a cigarette? Please!" I called out after finishing off one of the bottles of water.

One of the guards approached. He lit one and handed it to me. I know cigarettes are not good for you but at that moment it felt like the best thing in the world.

I tried hard to find a comfortable place to sit, but the insects were mauling me. Then after a couple of hours, the guard came back over and gave me a packet of 20 Benson & Hedges. I thought to myself maybe some of these guys do have a heart.

"Can I get a lighter?"

"No lighter."

"How can I light my cigarettes then?"

Perhaps he thought I would set fire to the hut. He lit my first cigarette and told me that I would not get any more cigarettes until the next day. He told me that all the guards had lighters, so all I had to do was ask one of them for a light when I needed one

"Make that packet last you until tomorrow."

I was unsure if they would give me any more cigarettes at all. As darkness set in, I began to wonder where, when and how this nightmare was going to end. I was too scared to sleep. The combination of ants, mosquitoes, snakes and half stoned pirates had me terrified, so sleep was the last thing on my mind

Lying on a bare plank of wood was not very comfortable either. The cigarettes were my distraction and they were getting hammered. I smoked them right down to the raw filter, enjoying every lingering draw. One of the nightshift guards also smoked and I cadged one or two of his for a while. I kept my pack firmly in my pocket so he did not see them. He did not know I had them until I asked him for a light. It was a very long first night and in the gloom I could see the ants crawling everywhere.

The morning sunshine broke into the clearing on my second day in captivity. I still had nothing to eat. I asked for food and was told by Thomas that they would get me chicken and rice later that day. He said they would be going to the village after they had had their baths.

I was surviving on my body's surges of adrenalin and bursts of nicotine. I asked the Elder Brother for a pack of cigarettes and he gave me another packet of Benson & Hedges.

"I prefer my St Moritz, can you get me some of them?" I asked rather brazenly.

He nodded and said he would buy me a carton of 200 St Moritz Menthol with his own money when he went to the village that day. I was a little unsure if he could get my brand of cigarettes if his village was only a small village? Going by my past experiences, St Moritz were only available in the larger villages. He passed me a lighter and made me promise just to use it to light my cigarettes. This was a step forward. I didn't have to ask for a light every time I wanted a fag. Again this was another of my attackers showing some compassion – was I winning some of them over? It looked like I was on the right track.

Later that day the Elder came back from the village. Lo and behold, true to his word, he handed me a carton of St Moritz menthol. He also put a case of bottled water on the ground at the side of my wooden bed. The cigarettes were a life-saver for me and they helped me keep my sanity in that hellhole. There was still no food, however. When Thomas came in to my side of the hut I asked him where my chicken and rice was, he said that it would come later in the day. He had already been to the village so it was strange and upsetting that he had not brought the food with him. Again he asked if I would like some local food, although I was weak from the lack of food I could not eat the local food, the smell of it was making me feel funny and nauseous.

Cigarettes also helped me build a rapport with the gang. In the days that followed some were even coming in and taking my cigarettes. If the Elder was around and saw them he would shout at them. They just grinned and shrugged their shoulders. My view was that smiling pirates smoking your fags are more inclined to keep you alive. For some strange reason at that time the cigarettes were as important to me as the water. It was a weird feeling to think of cigarettes as my only friend, but they brought me comfort and kept me going. When I had a cigarette, I seemed to be able to calm down a bit, helped me think straighter and allowed me to try to work these guys out and make some sort of plan in my mind.

That second morning I overheard one of the pirates saying in pidgin English that they had taken a million Naira from the tanker. It was becoming clear to me that some of the junior members of the gang were not receiving the same share of the cash as the senior members, as it was the junior members who were coming in for the cigarettes. As I did not receive any food at all, the water and the cigarettes were the only things I had to look forward to for the foreseeable future.

As I dragged on another fag, I thought about Helen, my wife, and our family in Scotland.

Helen was born and bred in Northfield Aberdeen, where she attended Northfield academy. I got to know Helen when she was friends with my sister. After some years when Helen had moved house from one area of Northfield to another, we became neighbours and lived only a couple of streets apart.

At one of the New Year's Day parties in my Sister's house in 1974 Helen and I met again, and started dating a few weeks after the party. We found we had a lot in common, especially our love of country and western music. After several dates we moved in together and then got married in 1976. We had both been married before and were both a little apprehensive about how it might work. I had two children from my first marriage and Helen had three children from her first marriage. I know it was very difficult at times for Helen coping with two different families when I was away from home for so long. Helen turned out to be a wonderful mother to all 5 children, and there was the normal family rows and argument to cope with. Helen bore the brunt of all this. Since the kids have grown up they have all become very close and they are all married now with children of their own. Helen is the only mother that my two children to my first marriage have. They never talk about their birth mother. Helen is a wonderful person with loads of character, being the wife of a seaman is not easy for any woman. Seamen's wives are a special breed and Helen is in a league of her own.

In all the years we have been married, she has had to deal with lots of problems on her own and has excelled in them all. When the kids attended both secondary and then high school Helen worked as well. She would get the kids off to school in the morning and then go to work. In our early years of marriage she worked at the Imperial Hotel in Aberdeen as a bar manageress, where she was in charge of the bar and lunchtime meals. She had to make sure the food was served on time and that the service was good. The Imperial Hotel was a very busy hotel in those days, they had a lot of clientele that were involved in the oil industry. She would finish at half past two each day and then return home for the kids coming home from school. Helen loved looking after the kids and she also loved working, you could not stop her, and obviously her salary as well as mine helped us give the kids a better quality of life.

After a number of years in Aberdeen we moved to a small village 14 miles north east of Aberdeen called Kemnay. The kids moved school and Helen changed jobs to be closer to home and the kids' school, she went to work in the local brick factory, working on a production line putting the bricks into the machine for painting. When we moved from Kemnay to Brechin, which is 11 miles north of Dundee and 35 miles south of Aberdeen, Helen found another job immediately. She went to work in the canning factory that produced tinned veg. Helen worked the machine that put the labels on the cans. She was kept very busy, and after working for most of the day she would come home and look after the kids and do her housework. How she managed is anybody's guess, I was away from home for long periods of time which makes Helen's achievements even more remarkable. After the kids left home we started to go line dancing together and had a good social life when I was home on leave. As I was not at home very often and only for short periods of time I could not get time to learn the dances, so I used to practice in the ship's wheelhouse. My crew were amazed at their captain practising line dancing on the bridge. I used to play the piece of music for each dance and would follow the steps on the dance sheet until I had perfected the dance. I would only practice the dances in the evenings when there were watch keepers on the bridge and all my paperwork was done. The looks on my watch keepers' faces when I was doing these dances were amazing, they wondered what was going on, and were hilarious when they tried to join in.

In 2014, Helen is 69 years of age and she now works in the cafeteria at the Asda store in Arbroath. She just loves working and loves the company of other people – a really amazing woman.

# 8

# ONBOARD TENSION
# AND THREATS OF POISONING

As I sat in my make-shift hut, swatting the flies and getting constantly bitten, scratching the sores and rashes that were appearing on my skin, there was no cream to treat these injuries and not enough water to pour over them to calm the itching down. I was even spitting on my fingers and rubbing my skin to see if this would help. The lumps and rashes on my skin were getting worse each day. I tried to tell the pirates how bad it was and even showed them the rashes but they did nothing except say they would contact a doctor to visit me in the jungle, which obviously never happened.

As I watched the antics of these gregarious Nigerian pirates with their guns, I tried to work out why this situation should have deteriorated so badly for this group of men. I am a working class guy brought up in Aberdeen. Sure, there was often drink-fuelled trouble with fishermen when they arrived back after a spell at sea. It was usually sorted by a spell in the Grampian police cells and a visit to the sheriff courts. There were bad apples but in general there was respect for the law. I've always believed in doing a fair day's work and getting paid fairly for that work.

Looking back on those early days as master of the *St Patrick* there were cultural issues that had to be dealt with, and to this day this will always be the case. When the *St Patrick* was ready to get back to work, Tony gathered the team to explain our job. We were working on an Esso pipeline that ran from the pumping station onshore to a single point mooring a mile and a half out in the bay where tankers hooked up to collect the oil. The pipeline on the seabed was bending and there was a serious risk of the line rupturing. Our job was to use our divers to pack the underside of the pipeline with sand bags. The deck crane would lift the sand bags down to the seabed where the divers could push them under the pipeline. In the meantime, some of the pipe would have to be airlifted to keep it straight while the bags were packed underneath. We also had an American representative from Esso on board to see what we were doing. There was no diving in the dark, so Tony explained there was a mooring buoy close to the job site where we would anchor at nights.

I was in the wheelhouse as we sailed at 6am out to the job site. We had to dodge a fleet of small fishing boats with no real sea sense as we cleared the entrance to the harbour. They came so close, that it would have been easy to hit them. We picked our way through this very carefully. I did not want an accident on my first day. Out on the job, we found that the wind picked up at roughly 1pm each day. The local African coastal breeze as the sea warmed up made the seas very choppy, causing a lot of movement on the barge. It was far too dangerous for our divers to work. For a few days we tied up at the mooring buoy, then Tony decided that because we were only 30 minutes' steam from the harbour we would head back to port each day. Most days we docked and every morning we sailed out from the harbour, dodging the same reckless fishing boats. In the beginning, all was quiet between the Nigerian and the Ghanaian crew members, then there were bouts of stealing, with cash and food disappearing. Some guys were caught red-handed and disciplined but somehow we never managed to crack the scam wide open. I started to see the risks the African crew were willing to take to subsidise their drinking ashore in the bush bars. There were continual bouts of bad conduct and this was difficult to control. We hired a guy called Eamon, a specialist crane driver from Ghana. He was a nice old man and very competent. In working mode, the crane operator is in his cab and has control over the deck crew. He is responsible for all the heavy lifting operations, and provides vital support for the divers. He can halt the job if he feels that lifting a load is not possible, too heavy or people are in danger. Eamon began having problems with the Nigerian boson called Levi, a very tall and powerful guy. I was beginning to find that many Nigerians could be rather aggressive in their manner and Levi was one of them. Eamon was unhappy and reported Levi for constant verbal harassment and grief. Levi was not interested in doing what he was told or what was required, and this had a knock-on effect with the other Nigerian deck crew. The Ghanaians were unhappy with the way Eamon was being treated, and Eamon was clearly shaken and upset. We had to reprimand Levi, warning him that if his behaviour did not improve we would be forced to send him home and get a replacement boson. I was one of the ship's masters, it was my job to keep order and safety on the vessel, but the growing sense of belligerence, with no respect for rank whatsoever was completely new to me.

After two months working on the pipeline, I prepared for my first leave. I was looking forward to seeing Helen and telling her all about my first African experience. I had my holdall packed when a group of Nigerians and Ghanaians approached me. I thought they had come to say goodbye and wish me a safe trip.

"What are you going to bring back for us?" asked one of them.

"What do you mean?" I said rather naively.

"Our presents. We want some nice gifts from you when you come back," was the reply.

They were like children expecting Santa Claus and they were deadly serious. Tony told me to ignore them. In hindsight, perhaps I should have taken his advice.

I witnessed scenes of deep poverty on my return trip to Accra from Sekondi. It made my heart sink just seeing the desperate state of so many people living in rags at the side of the road. I had five weeks' leave at home with Helen, where she spoiled me with her home cooking, including wonderful plates of her mince, tatties and skirlie. Then I returned for my second spell with the *St Patrick* to complete the job with Esso Ghana.

In October 2002, we stayed in Ghana to refit a quayside. The barge was in dire need of maintenance all round. We decided that we should keep the Nigerian deck and catering crew on board to help with the various tasks, although we did not have another contract. During this refit and indeed during the whole Ghanaian contract, we had more personnel problems. The behaviour of one able seaman called Tony became so bad that Paul Partridge, our chief engineer and chief electrician complained to me and said he could not work with him any longer. We had no choice but to sack Tony and send him back to Nigeria. But the atmosphere on board was becoming charged.

It was approaching Christmas and I was preparing to go home, leaving Paul in charge on board with five Nigerian crew members. I took the crew to the bush bar to buy them a few beers before heading off the next morning. As the beers flowed the Nigerians started to tell me that it was wrong to sack Tony. They became heated and said the chief engineer instigated his sacking for no reason. Chillingly, they told me that while Paul was alone with them on board they would deal with him.

"What do you mean? I hope this isn't some kind of threat," I told the guys as they sipped their large glasses of beer.

"It will be an accident, Captain. It might be something that he eats that doesn't agree with him," one said.

"That is enough. You are all out of order. I will not listen to talk like this. Tony got himself sacked by his own disobedient behaviour, it was nothing to do with Paul."

In the short time I had been in West Africa I had heard horror stories of how Africans dealt with someone whom they thought had wronged them and they did not like. A favourite method is to poison their victims. And I knew these particular guys were certainly capable of poisoning Paul when there was no one else around. With the poor medical system in Africa, even after an autopsy, nobody would be any the wiser and Paul would be dead. I was learning about the ways of African people. These guys were normally quite nice guys but when someone upset them they showed a different type of attitude. I changed the subject and bought some last beers before we went back to the *St Patrick*. I could not sleep that night. I knew I had to tell Paul and warn him of the dangers, but I was fearful that Paul would then confront them. Next day, I told Paul the whole story and he called them all on deck. He warned them that he would go to the police and have them arrested for threatening to kill him. This made the guys panic as they knew in Africa that the police looked at a threat as bad as the crime itself. I said the police would not be brought in, if the guys promised to behave and stop holding a grudge against Paul. They nodded their approval. A tricky situation was averted and Paul and I struck up a great friendship. Even in November 2014 Paul is trying his best to help me get over my terrible ordeal all the way from Australia. Paul has just suffered a terrible tragedy in losing his young son to cancer and yet still finds the time to help me. Paul is a very special friend.

With no work after the refit in Ghana, our instructions were to take the vessel back around the Gulf of Guinea to the Kent Base in the Bonny River in Nigeria. We kept the marine crew of Nigerians for the journey which took us about ten days. My Nigerian experiences were about to really kick in.

# 9

# BEATING BANDITS ON THE BONNY RIVER

It is wrong to paint a stereotype of a whole nation. But if I didn't enjoy meeting, working and socialising with the vast majority of Nigerians I had the fortune to meet I would never have spent so long in the country. Yes,they can be loud and aggressive, they can cut corners when a job needs done, they will disappear to the corner of a large vessel when hands are needed, and they can be extremely bad mannered and ill-tempered. Yet somehow there is a wonderful joy and gregarious love of life that exudes from so many of them. They can be like puppies laughing, joking and smiling and showing incredible loyalty to the vessel, but things can turn very quickly and you need all the skills of a proper man manager, particularly at sea. I knew how to run a vessel like the *St Patrick*, but the cultural aspect of working with Africans was an extra dimension. After some time and TLC towards them I managed to gain their trust and most of us became like family.

We arrived at the pilot station at the entrance to the Bonny River at 6am. This is close to the great Niger Delta, which runs through Central Africa from Timbuktu and spills out into the Gulf of Guinea. By the time it meets the sea it is a dark reddish torrent filled with sand and silt from inland Africa. At Bonny, we gave our vessel's details and we were told to continue up the river to our base near Port Harcourt – Nigeria's sprawling city in the wetlands at the mouth of the delta. There were very strong tides against us most of the way up river and it took us five and a half hours to reach Kent Resources Base, near Rumuolumeni. It was mid-afternoon by the time we docked and I went to meet John Weir, the PW base manager, for the first time. He was another great Irishman. I also met the Kent Base staff and was introduced to the private police officers of Mopol, who were a group of untrained guys that had been given guns and uniforms and were called private police, but they were recognised by the government. Mopol had their own quarters in the camp.

This was also where I first met Alabo, my driver, and little did I know then the major role he would play in saving my life at a later date. Alabo was over six feet in height and built like a heavyweight boxer. With his wife and daughters he lived in a very small two-room house without electricity and running water. Alabo turned out to be very loyal to me and would do anything for me. I could call him at any time and he would be with me ASAP. I used to give Alabo tips every time we went out, he was delighted with this and said that some of the tips I gave him was more than a week's salary. Alabo was earning about 5,000 Naira per week then, which was about £20. He told me that the tips I was giving him all went towards his family's upkeep. Alabo and his family could not thank me enough. I used to take back presents for Alabo and his family every time I went on leave. Helen would even come to the shops with me and we would pick the presents together.

The base had its own jetty and was secured by large concrete walls with a barbed wire fence round the top. It was really like a fortress. There were large iron entrance gates with a small guard house where everyone had to check in and out. On my second day I was introduced to the owner of PW Group, Hugo Flinn, who founded the business. He was an elderly man from Cork in his mid-80s and deeply proud of his Irish history and heritage. His father had been a parliamentary secretary to the Irish leader Eamon de Valera, and his business had undertaken a lot of public works in Ireland. They build roads all over Ireland and also work at airports when there are new runways required.

Beside Kent Base there was a wonderful stretch of clean white sand which was being dug up, collected and sold. Just outside the gates and down the road, toward the village at Aker there were stalls, shops and the now-familiar bush bars. Nearby, at Rumuolumeni, the Italian energy company Saipem also had a massive fabrication and construction yard. The company employed over 3,000 people in Nigeria alone, including 500 expats, and had a living complex with its offices and a large social club inside a secure compound. I met quite a lot of the Saipem expat workers and we would receive invitations into the club at the weekends. In those early days, if we wanted a beer or a packet of cigarettes, we would just walk to the village.

One afternoon the situation changed for the worse. Alabo was driving me into Port Harcourt, about two miles from our base, so I could do some shopping. Ten minutes into the journey we came upon a body lying on the side of the road. Alabo slowed up, and I rolled down my window for a closer inspection. Lying in the dust was a black male and next to him there was a splattering of crimson blood seeping into the earth. The body was headless. I simply could not believe what I was seeing. I was shocked, I had never seen anything like this before. A couple of hundred yards from this corpse was a church. Sticking out of the top of a large pole, there was a human head. I was almost sick. I had to turn my head away and not look. I asked Alabo why this had happened, he said it was a ritual killing but would not elaborate. I still do not understand what he meant by a ritual killing. For days, the body lay on the side of the road. Nobody would move it. Nobody dared. The police knew it was there but did nothing about it. In the days that followed, the body started to smell and rot. It was just a fly-covered meat carcass being picked at by large birds. We normally drove with the two front windows down, so we could have a cigarette, but as the body continued to decompose Alabo would tell me to wind my window up every time we passed. After more than a week the body and the head on the stick, were taken away by a disposal unit.

One Friday night I decided to go into Port Harcourt for a beer or two. It had been a very busy week on board, cleaning and painting the vessel and I had to get away from the fumes of paint for a few hours. It had been peaceful for a while so I thought it would be quite safe. Plenty of expats headed into town on a Friday night, so I asked Alabo to pick me up at 7pm to take me to the Cheers Bar. I would take Alabo into the bar to join me for a soft drink and we would just chat. Cheers had two large bars inside and one very large seating area outside, where there were live rock and reggae bands at the weekend. It would be a change of scene for us. Most of the expats prefer their drivers to sit outside in the cars and wait for them. I like to treat everyone as I would like to be treated myself, so Alabo was invited in with me. This built a mutual bond that would later prove to be vital in my release from the kidnappers. We went into the outdoor bar, found a table and sat down. The band was loud but played a tight set of rock music with some couples dancing and swaying at the front.

Alabo and I were there for about an hour when all of a sudden we heard a ruckus outside and saw the doormen running and bolting the gates. The band stopped playing and people began standing up. Several loud gunshots reverberated in the still night and someone shouted that there were militants in the street outside. There was a secret exit at the back and as Alabo had parked in a quiet back street, we decided to get out, just in case the militants forced their way inside. There was a sharp exit as the whole outside bar cleared of people. By the time we reached the car other escaping expats had the same idea. Moments later we heard police sirens at the front and we knew that the militants would now make a run for it. The Nigerian police do not mess about. They shoot to kill and do not care who gets in their way.

Alabo drove back to Kent Base. The road was quite busy as a lot of expats were fleeing the scene of the incident, Alabo explained that these guys were basically just armed robbers and were looking for easy money from the expats, and that they would have kidnapped some of the expats given the chance. He also told me, if the police had not intervened, the attackers would have robbed the bar as well. Apart from the large volume of traffic trying to overtake each other and occasionally giving the odd car a nudge out of the way, the journey back went without incident and we did not see any sign of the attackers. Inside the gate we had a beer at the bar to calm us down. All our armed guards were there and we felt safe. What I did not know at the time was that kidnapping was reaching epidemic proportions and between 2006 and 2008 an estimated $100 million was paid out in ransoms in Nigeria.

I got my first sign of corruption in the wheelhouse of the *St Patrick*. We would get regular visits from Nigerian immigration and customs officers and because of this I would spend days after arriving from sea diligently making sure the vessel and the paperwork was up to date. When the immigration officers came on board they wanted to see all the crew's documents. I kept all passports and visas locked in my safe in the cabin and brought them to the wheelhouse. The officers would argue about every passport and visa and be on board for hours. There were always at least four of them. I could argue with them until I was blue in the face but my arguments fell on deaf ears. When they were finished their inspections they would ask what I had for them. We always received local currency from the office just for this sort of thing. It did not matter how much I offered them, it was never enough. Most of the time I had to tell them that what I had offered was all the Naira I had on board. Then they would ask where the dollars were, when I told them we did not carry dollars they didn't believe me and said that every vessel carried dollars. This was a very similar thing said by the pirates when they attacked my vessel, did this mean that all Nigerians were the same? Or was it just coincidence?

This was normal life in Nigeria and it became deeply tiresome and annoying. I was always glad to see them go and did not relish their next visit. I had to go through the exact same rigmarole with the customs officers. It would always cost us money even though I made sure everything was in order. If I did not go along with them they would get angry and threaten to have me arrested. They made no attempt to hide the fact that they were corrupt. John Weir was as frustrated as I was but said corruption was commonplace in Nigeria. It was something that the company just had to deal with. It must cost British companies and those from other countries working in Nigeria a fortune in public relations money.

After a few weeks waiting for an offshore contract, it was time again to go home on leave. I got my second lesson on Nigerian corruption when I arrived at the international airport in Port Harcourt. I like wearing jewellery and I normally have on five rings, two neck chains, a good watch, three gold bracelets and a gold earring. It had certainly attracted attention over the years but wearing this gold jewellery in Nigeria had never been a problem until now. The immigration officers and the customs officers asked for an item of my jewellery. I told them that my wife had bought me the jewellery as a present. So they then asked me for money saying if I did not give them something they would delay me from travelling. Others in the queue could plainly see and hear what was going on, but the officers simply did not care. I stumped up some spare notes just to get through the barrier. The begging by the crew and the workers at the base for presents from me went on and on. On this trip, I relented. I was asked to bring back portable DVD players, original football shirts and mobile telephones. When I arrived home I explained to Helen about the requests. She thought I was crazy and did not like it, but she helped me buy the presents from Argos and Tesco. It cost quite a lot of money. It was a rod for my own back. Once I started this habit, everyone wanted a piece of the action too. Because I had given so many presents how could I say no now? So the buying of presents went on until every one of my crew had a present, including the office staff as well. I thought this might bring some peace. Despite our generosity, one day I had money and my mobile phone stolen out of my cabin while we were at sea. It had to be one of my crew – there was no one else on board. That evening I emailed Helen about the incident and she could not believe that one of my crew could be so callous after all that we had done for them, but I suppose you get this type of thing in other walks of life as well. Helen suggested I pay the money I would have used to buy gifts into a children's charity in Nigeria, where the money would be appreciated. I decided not to buy any more presents.

News came through that we had a new contract for the *St Patrick*. It would be back to work again – and I was looking forward to this. Kent Resources, now PW Nigeria, would be returning to Nigeria, working in the narrow creeks between Escravos and Wari, on a new subsea power and communication cable laid for Shell between the power station and the villages scattered around the Shell power station. After the cable was laid and commissioned, Shell decided to get a dredger in to deepen the river channel. The dredger had a local Nigerian Master and he carelessly took his vessel right through the middle of this expensive cable. It sliced the cable in two. The cable had thousands of fibreoptic wires wrapped inside, so we had two telecoms experts on board from British Telecom in London. They were both getting £500 per day: double my day rate at the time.

We were increasingly anxious about working in these creeks due to the recent conflicts and flare-ups close to Wari but the security advisors assured us that all would be fine. The job required two captains on board, myself and a lad called Greg Caldecott, who had been on board the *St Patrick* for some time and was treated as No. 1 Captain by the crew. Paul Partridge and I arrived at the work site and had to go through the normal procedures of meetings and paying off all of the surrounding communities. On board, we also had a rep from Kent Resources and another from Shell who handled the negotiations and the pots of money handed to the local communities.

A steady stream of small boats, often with several families on the deck, came alongside as we went past each rural community. Apart from their daily pay-out, they begged for food, water and cigarettes. We didn't refuse because it might agitate them and could cause us all sorts of problems. Shell were desperate to get this job done, there was no way we could afford delays. It was a pest having to deal with this every day whilst trying to get the job done as soon as possible. There was no way we could not let them on board. We set the *St Patrick* up on DP above the point where the cable was sliced in two. The divers were deployed to make sure we were in the correct position, and once this was confirmed and we had a lifting bridle attached to both ends of the cut cable we proceeded to lift the ends on board with the hired deck crane. We had constructed a hut on the stern where BT's fibreoptic technicians could repair the cable in the shade. One cable end was lifted on the starboard side and the other end lifted on the port side. Both ends were taken into the hut through flaps on the side of the hut and placed on a work bench. Every day I dropped in to watch the telecom guys and check on the progress. The thin coloured fibreoptic cables were minute and there were thousands of them. The guys had special tools and glasses to carry out the work. The job went quite well apart from when the propellers become fouled up due to the rubbish floating about in the dirty river. We completed the job in 14 days which was considered very good by Shell due to the extensive damage of the cable. As we had been operating on DP for the duration, it had been quite stressful and we were looking forward to a few satisfying beers in Forcados while demobbing the equipment. Sometimes there was equipment on board from the company that gave us the contract which had to go back.

We were boarded by a local pilot and headed down the narrow creeks towards Forcados. As we steamed slowly towards Forcados, some guys came alongside in a canoe, and pulled themselves up onto our deck. We did not see the intruders until they were on board, but they brandished hand-guns. They slapped a couple of the crew around in the mess and the next thing the intruders were up in the bridge shouting and screaming.

"Do as we tell you! Slow the boat down! Slow the boat down!"

The pilot shifted our controls to dead slow, although the *St Patrick*, being a large barge, was a slow-coach in the water anyway.

"What's up? Put those guns down. What do you want?" I said.

"We want our money. You've not paid our local people for coming here. Give us the money. We want five million Naira."

One of the Kent Resources reps bravely stood firm and told them this just wasn't possible.

"Look guys, it's Friday and the office is closed now. But the company guarantees to pay you on Monday."

"No. No. Money now!"

"You heard the rep, he's telling you the truth. If you want your money, leave now and you can collect on Monday," I said sternly.

The *St Patrick* was still moving slowly toward the dock at Forcados and I wondered if we could call in the Nigerian Navy to come and evict them, this was a long shot as they would and could have stopped us using our radios or mobile phones.

"You better get off now – or we will call the Navy in."

Finally, they got the message and left the vessel. They would wait for their payment on Monday.

We docked at Forcados, cleared customs and immigration and I completed all the paperwork. The crew broke down all the gear ready to demob the next day and Shell placed armed Nigerian Navy guards on board. Paul and I went to the local Lamnalco bush bar to have a few beers. It was quite a relief.

During the weekend the company rep told us that Kent Resources management said they were not going to pay out any more money, certainly not to the young guys who boarded our boat. This didn't go down well when the raiders radioed in to us. The would-be pirates shouted and threatened us again demanding their money. When you use the radios the port authorities and other vessels listening on the channel you are transmitting on can hear the conversation – in fact anyone within a 25 mile radius, tuned into the same channel can hear you. We were hoping that the navy or police were listening and would perhaps intervene.

"You will not be able to leave for Port Harcourt, unless we get our money. Have it ready," they warned over the radio.

The *St Patrick* was due to sail on Monday morning. Greg made a rather fool-hardy decision, without consulting me or Paul. He was going to sail without naval security guards on board because they were too expensive. When Paul and I heard this, we refused to sail under such conditions. We knew the armed pirates would return possibly bringing a stronger force, if we did not have guards on board.

Greg accused us of being mutineers, which made Paul and I howl with laughter.

"Me, a mutineer? You're having a laugh!" Paul and I said in unison.

After contacting the office, it was agreed that security guards would be paid for so we could sail back to Port Harcourt. Greg was harassed and probably scared like the rest of us, but he made another big mistake. He set the sailing time and ordered the pilot. I double-checked the local tides against his sailing time and discovered we were going to sail in low water. This was dangerous as we had to cross over several sand banks to get out to sea. I told Paul and showed him the chart, and we both went to Greg and the pilot. They simply would not listen. What could we do? We decided to let them both get on with it, after all Greg's name was on the paperwork. If anything happened it was the fault of both Greg and the pilot.

We set sail and Paul and I both made sure we were watching events from the bridge. Greg was not DP qualified, so I put the vessel into manual DP so as the vessel would handle better. I had the steering controls of the vessel as we made our way through the tree-lined creeks. The radio crackled. It was the pirates wanting us to stop and give them money. But we were steaming away from them now.

We approached the sand banks which were now clearly visible above the water. There were flocks of sea birds pecking for insects and worms along the sand. We were heading straight for the middle of this strand of grey sand. Greg and the pilot both panicked when they realised their error. We were in great danger. Along this stretch of water there were terrible tidal streams running, pushing the vessel onto the sand. If we grounded, we could easily sink. We could all lose our lives. Although we were crossing sand banks we were quite a distance from the coastline, the tidal force here was extreme, if any of us went into the water we would have been dragged away with the tides and would have little or no chance of surviving. I had to act quickly and decisively, forcing the *St Patrick* hard to starboard away from the bank, while Paul shouted out the water depths from the local chart. Our own sonar showed we were less than a metre from touching the bottom. It was very hairy and extremely close. Between us, we managed to get the vessel safely back into a deeper water channel. Greg and the pilot stood silent and ashen-faced. Where this pilot had gotten his licence from was anybody's guess.

With the vessel safe and the scare over, Paul and I started swearing at the two guys, in relief more than anger.

"What the hell were you doing? You could have killed us all going onto that sandbank against that tide. That was the most reckless piece of seamanship I have ever seen," said Paul to Greg and the pilot.

"You were shown the charts and the time of the tide. Yet you ignored that information. This was highly irresponsible. You put us all in danger!" I shouted.

They both stood like scolded schoolboys and said nothing. The ship's radio was crackling with more threats. For a moment, we'd actually forgotten about the pirates tailing us.

"We know where you are, we can see you. Bring us our money or we come and get you. Stop your vessel or you will be in big trouble," warned the pirates on the radio.

We cranked the *St Patrick* up to full speed, but it was a lumbering craft, creating a large amount of swell in the creeks and was unable to out-run any pirates in speed-boats. The radio crackled again.

"Give us our money. You're bad for putting armed navy guards on board. We know your boat – if you return we will get you all," came a half-hearted threat.

We were now out in the open sea and on our way back to Port Harcourt and although the pirates followed for a while, there were no further incidents and we managed to reach our destination without drama. When the managers heard about our escapade, Greg was in the bad books.

Over the following three years, work became increasingly intermittent as the *St Patrick* was only getting the odd contract.

In my view it was not being properly marketed as a workhorse for the oil industry. The people running the vessel didn't have a marine background, so they couldn't really sell our services and reliability.

I went home in early 1996 for a few months. During this time I decided to have a break in the sun and moved to Spain with Helen. We gave up our house and everything that went with it for a clean break from our lives in Scotland. Helen had been on holiday there a few times when I was at sea. It was a wonderful place to go and recharge the batteries and we had a grand group of expat friends enjoying the sun and sangria lifestyle. We had family and friends living in a small town called Calpe, not far from Benidorm. When we first moved to Calpe we moved in with our son, his wife and two kids. He had quite a large house with a spare bedroom for us. We lived there for a few months until we bought our own house not far from our son and his family.

I had a friend who owned a big car dealership in Spain, with offices in Calpe, Benidorm and Alicante. As I was having a break and had plenty of spare time on my hands he asked if I would like the odd job of delivering and collecting cars for him. I agreed and he called me when I was required. The more I did for him the more he called, in fact he kept me quite busy, and so I did not get much time with Helen to enjoy the sun. I used to deliver and pick up cars all over Spain. I would even take right hand drive cars to England and take left hand drive cars back when they were available. I drove some top of the range cars, I even drove a left hand drive Aston Martin from England to Spain. Most of our spare time in Spain was spent in Benidorm line dancing.

After 10 years in Spain, Helen said that she had had enough of the sun and wanted to return to Scotland, so we sold up and moved back home.

In 2005, a new managing director (Chris Woolley) arrived

at the PW Base in Port Harcourt and began turning the business around. Chris is a very tall man and well built, he is great to get on with and we formed a friendship immediately. He lived with his wife and two children in England. Chris came from an engineering background and had already worked in Nigeria for quite a number of years, he was a general manager with a Nigerian owned company, and he was like the owner's right hand man. This was where Chris learned his man management skills with Nigerians. He was well versed in Nigerian culture which would serve him well at a later date when he had to deal and negotiate with my attackers.

I was driving with Helen from England to Scotland to visit family when Hugh Lynch, one of the PW overseas big shots, called me and asked if I would go back to Nigeria and re-join the *St Patrick*. He told me that Chris Woolley was now in charge and that things would be different. This time the vessel would have permanent long-term project work. So I decided to return to Nigeria where I met Chris for the first time and we have been very good friends ever since. He is a hard-working and methodical guy who gets things done properly and fairly. He managed to get the vessel a contract for a trial period with Exxon Mobil Nigeria in the Qua Iboe Oilfield. This was a breakthrough for all of us. To celebrate, Chris and I decided to go for some dinner and a few drinks at a Chinese restaurant in Port Harcourt. Alabo picked me up at 8pm to meet with Chris at the restaurant an hour later. As the restaurant was at the other end of the town we had to take the highway. We were stuck in heavy traffic and travelling at a snail's pace. It was obvious that we were going to be late, so I called Chris to put him in the picture. We were just about a couple of miles from the restaurant when there were several large lightning flashes and loud percussive bangs in front of us in the distance. Immediately, all the cars in front veered onto the central reservation in the middle of the highway and began U-turning in the opposite direction. Alabo kept going forward slowly for a few more metres whilst craning his neck out the front window. Suddenly we were the only car on an empty highway heading in this direction. The bangs and flashes were still getting closer and louder. Alabo turned the car round. We crossed the middle aisle very carefully until we were on the other side of the highway joining a stream of vehicles. We then sped back in the opposite direction. There were loads of cars with the same idea, we were not sure at the time what the problem was, but the important thing was to get out of there ASAP as there was still gunfire and flashing lights behind us. We managed to get back to the safety of the base without further incident. We heard later that the militants were on the prowl again in the town and were shooting at cars and throwing hand grenades. Most of these incidents were political and involved the Nigerian people and their government, but as an expat you do not want to get caught up in this.

Chris and I both worked our socks off to get the vessel up to scratch, making changes and suitable updates. Exxon Mobil came to do an audit and vessel inspection and we passed with flying colours. We did such a good job sorting everything out that the *St Patrick* is still under contract for Exxon Mobil to this day (November 2014), although she is now owned by a different company. When working for Exxon Mobil in Nigeria there were a lot of incidents that did not seem right. When Exxon first went to Nigeria it was run by American managers and everything was done by the book. As the Americans handed over the top jobs, more Nigerians were in charge and you could see a gulf in culture. The organisation was poor and they did not adhere to the safety rules and regulations, even the ones they made themselves. When the Americans were in charge, safety was paramount, but after they left safety was very often compromised. We thought that the Nigerians did not know any better, yet they did, but chose to skirt around the rules when it suited them. For example, on a DP vessel there are distinct rules of operation that you have to adhere to which are all laid down by the International Marine Contractors Association, (IMCA). IMCA is a trade association representing the companies and organisations operating offshore and they have been the champions for better regulations and integrity for working at sea. I uphold these recommendations and guidelines and all British vessels take the recommendations very seriously. In Nigeria, it was completely different. One of the recommendations is that a DP vessel should never go up wind towards a platform in breezy weather. The reason for this is if the wind is blowing the vessel onto the platform and the DP system fails, you will drift onto the platform. If you are downwind of the platform and anything happens the vessel will drift away from the platform. A lot of the Exxon platforms did not have cranes on either side of the platform. So inevitably the platform control room operators would ask us to go up close alongside, often when the weather was rough and coming from the wrong direction. At first we refused and told them the rules but they did not understand. There would be arguing and shouting at us over the radio. While we stuck by our guns they would report us to the Onshore Marine Vessel Coordinator. Their bosses would call up asking us what the problem was. We would politely explain the rules. They tried to be understanding but told us the lifts were very important and the *St Patrick* was the only vessel that could carry this work out. We still resisted. This would increase their irritation and we would be reported to our own office. Thankfully, our bosses would support us saying that the captains were the company's representatives at sea. If we thought something was not safe, then we should not do it, but if we thought conditions were good enough to do the lifts it was up to the captains to decide. In the end, we decided to do the lifts but only in calm weather and no heavy tides. We had confidence in our own ability and in the capabilities of the vessel.

Most of the control room operators on the platforms in Nigeria had never been to sea and knew absolutely nothing regarding the rules and regulations of the sea. Yet they were prepared to argue with the vessels' captains. This became a constant battle. I regularly took a stance and refused to do a job if the control room operator's attitude became too abusive. The Nigerians seemed to be in general, quite loud and abusive in manner, perhaps this was just their culture or upbringing, and the disrespect towards ship's captains and their officers, often operating in hazardous sea conditions, was the worst I have seen anywhere in the world. As I have said, I do not think they knew any better, it was just the way they were, sometimes they did not even realise they were being abusive and offensive.

While the offshore attitudes were truculent and at times resentful, with regards to piracy it wasn't until 2008 that things took a turn for the worse in our region of Nigeria. Through the grapevine, we heard that piracy was on the increase offshore and getting ever closer to where we were working. Expats of all nationalities were being held-up, kidnapped onshore but were usually released very quickly. It came to a point around about 2011 that Exxon Mobil started operating a convoy system for any vessel working for them and going to port. Although they did not have any problems there were reports of vessels being attacked in the deeper waters off the entrance to the Bonny River. Over the next couple of years the kidnapping onshore and offshore became more frequent, people were obviously hearing that there was easy money to be made from mugging and kidnapping expats. Everybody seemed to jump at this chance of making easy money. It was widely known that ransoms were being paid. Yet, up until the time I was kidnapped there had been no other reported incidents of kidnapping in the Qua Iboe Oilfield.

# 10

# THE CHEAPNESS OF LIFE
# AND CRUELTY OF DEATH

My life was now on a knife edge. We are seldom confronted by
the shocking and often random nature of life and death. Many
of us live in a cocoon of comfort far removed from the harsh
reality of places such as Nigeria. In the UK, we take the rule of
law so much for granted, however, in Nigeria there is little or
no respect for the law. Life is less important than money, and
for whatever reason the Nigerian authorities are incapable or
uninterested in delivering justice.

I began to remember the sad story of one of our Nigerian
quarter masters called Levinus Barry, known as Barry. He was
a very good AB (deckhand), and had been on board for several
years during which time he kept himself to himself. He would
quietly get on with his work and would not be led astray. I liked
him a great deal. Although he started as an AB I was always
encouraging him to go and sit his Quarter master's certificate
as I felt sure he would do well in this position. A quarter master
is in charge of the ABs on deck when there is no other officer
present. He organises everything on deck, looking after the
lifting gear and the stores. He also looks after the paint store
and checks the vessel to make sure that everything is in order
and all the paintwork is kept up to scratch. Barry did eventually
go and sit his Quarter master's certificate and then returned to

us as an AB. I told him that I was very proud of him and to have patience – I was sure that a quarter master's position would become available for him soon. After about six months one of the quarter masters left to go and work on the oil platforms; he had been offered more money and would be able to spend more time at home. Our ABs worked four weeks on and two weeks off at that time, compared to the two weeks on and two weeks off on a platform. When I promoted Barry to quarter master, he was delighted and said he would never let me down. Barry sailed as quarter master for quite some time and turned out to be one of the best quarter masters we had ever had. Barry was married with four children and was only in his mid-thirties. He had inherited quite a lot of tribal land and his ambition was to build a house when he had saved enough money. I had heard from some of my crew that Barry's wife's family were jealous and were trying to get their hands on Barry's land.

On one trip Barry did not come back offshore with his normal crew change and we had to promote one of the ABs to quarter master. Jacob had only been with us for a short period of time but already had his Quarter master's certificate, and he had sailed with Captain Bob with his previous company. Bob Hales was my back-to-back, he had been my opposite number for seven years, and was very good as captain of the vessel. We worked very well together as back-to-backs. After the crew change I asked a couple of the Port Harcourt lads if they knew where Barry was and why he hadn't turned up for his spell at sea. The guys told me he was unwell and had been vomiting for the last week of his leave. He had gone to see a local doctor and was receiving native treatment. After a few weeks we received the shocking news that Barry had died. I wanted to know more about this. I knew the crew would know as they were always on their mobile phones whenever we were in range of a phone network. The story going around was that Barry had been poisoned and the gossip from the village was that his wife was involved somehow. Barry had been poisoned?! I asked the crew on board what they thought, they said that nothing would surprise them, and that was Nigeria for you. I asked if the police were investigating the incident and couldn't believe the answer I got. They all said that the police did not even get involved. Barry was lying in the morgue and nobody was interested in how he died. There was no post mortem or any autopsy, so there was no way of finding out the actual cause of death. I really missed Barry as he had been like one of my family.

We had another shock whilst we were in dry dock in Abidjan (Ivory Coast). Each morning I would chair the 'Tool-Box Talk'. All the crew were expected to attend, and we would discuss the work that had been done the day before and the schedule for that day. This day, Chris Woolley was on board as he had come to Abidjan as often as he could to get a progress report on the dry dock work. He would also have meetings with the Nigerian crew where he would be open to questions. He liked to make sure that everyone was happy.

I would go to the upper mess with the tool-box talk register and each guy would sign before we got started. Each head of department would give their report and I would write everything down for my daily report. I noticed that Remy Animoke, the ship's electrician and one of the permanent crew, was missing. I usually gave everyone ten minutes grace to get to the meeting yet still Remy had not shown up.

"Anyone seen Remy this morning? Was he in the mess hall for breakfast?" I asked.

There were several shakes of heads. No one had seen him.

"Was Remy out last night?" I inquired.

I knew he did not drink alcohol but enjoyed a stroll and a soft drink in the evening. Some of the guys said they had seen Remy the night before but thought he had come back to the *St Patrick* around midnight. I was keen to progress with the meeting and asked a couple of the crew to go and have a look in his cabin. Minutes later, they came back saying that the cabin was locked. This rang an alarm bell in my head. I had known Remy for a long time, Chris had known him even longer.

I went to the key locker to get the spare keys for Remy's cabin. Chris, myself and a couple of other crew members went down to the lower accommodation and tried putting the key in the lock. The key would not enter the key hole and it was then that we realised the door was locked from the inside. We were deeply worried now. There was a vent on the bottom of the door. I asked King Benard, the other on board electrician to get a screwdriver and take the vent off. He removed the vent but it was not large enough for anyone to pass though, but King got down on his belly and managed to look into the cabin which was in darkness. He was certain Remy was lying on the bed.

Chris and I were really alarmed now. King managed to get his hand up to the lock on the inside and managed to turn the key and open the door. We entered the cabin, turned on the light and Remy was indeed lying on the bed. His hands crossed on top of his chest. He looked very peaceful, and one of the guys gave his shoulders a shake. There was no response. I moved the guys out of the way and checked Remy's pulse. There was no pulse and Remy was not breathing. I tried to move Remy's arms but they were very stiff. It was obvious that Remy was dead and had been for some time now. I could not believe it and I told Chris to double-check Remy's pulse. He shook his head, there was no pulse, and Remy was indeed dead. There was no point in even trying CPR as Remy had been dead for quite some time and the body was stiff. We placed Remy's blanket over his whole body and I ordered everybody out of the cabin. I locked the door and told King to put the vent back on the door. We were all shocked and some of the crew were hysterical and were wailing and crying.

Remy's work mates had known him for years. Back in the upper mess we told the rest of the crew. Every one of them was crying. It was deeply sad. The crew were told there would be no work that day and to go to their cabins but to be available for interviews when the police and coroner arrived. We felt that the correct thing to do was to give them some time to themselves to pray for Remy and his family, which I was quite sure they would do. On the bridge I called the vessel's agent and explained what had happened. He passed on his condolences and said the correct procedure was to contact the Carena shipyard and they would take it from there. Within a couple of hours the police, the local hospital doctor, and immigration and vessel representatives were swarming all over the *St Patrick*. The police and doctor entered Remy's cabin and the doctor officially declared Remy dead. Immediate arrangements were made for an ambulance to take Remy's body to the local morgue. The doctor could not tell us what the cause of Remy's tragic death was. I had to do a full report for the police and they interviewed everyone on board that day. As Remy died on board the ship I had to make an entry in the vessel's official log book and this would be sent to St Vincent and Grenadines, the vessel's flag state. After the ambulance departed with Remy's body the police started their interviews. We were interviewed one by one with the vessel's shipping agent in attendance. I had to also be in attendance when each crew member was questioned. So it was a long and stressful day.

The police asked the crew if they were aware of anybody that had a grudge against Remy and how he got on with the people in the local village. We all presumed that poor Remy had just died in his sleep from natural causes but there was doubt in everybody's mind. Was there something sinister regarding Remy's death? Chris contacted Remy's family, he knew the family quite well anyway. Chris asked them if they wanted a postmortem and if they wanted to know how Remy had died. They agreed and Chris said he would arrange this. Everybody was on tenterhooks until the postmortem was carried out, confirming that Remy had died of natural causes. A massive heart attack in his sleep. Such a shame for such a young man with a young family.

Chris arranged for Remy's body to be shipped back to Nigeria where his family had arranged to have their loved one picked up. There is a strange custom in Nigeria regarding someone's death: the body can be held in cold storage for months before the burial. After Remy's body was shipped back to Nigeria I had to get all Remy's belongings together and make a list on my PC of every item. I signed it then gave it to the vessel's agent, and all his belongings were sent to Remy's family. I decided that we should have a collection from the crew on board and from the personnel on leave for Remy's family. We managed to get quite a good collection, mostly from the expats but his Nigerian crew mates donated what they could, and some of them even came to me for a salary advance so they could donate a little more.

A few days after Remy's death, the crew were back to work and seemed to be laughing and joking as if nothing had happened. Even King Benard, his best friend, didn't seem to take long to get over Remy's death. When the burial came none of the crew on board asked for leave to attend, although those on leave attended. I would have attended myself but as the master on board at the time I could not get time off from the vessel. Chris and the office staff attended the funeral. Chris said it was a very sad occasion.

About a week after his death it emerged that Remy had a serious problem with his blood pressure and instead of going to a hospital to see a proper doctor he went to see a witch doctor in his local village. It was such a waste of life: the crew said if Remy had seen a real doctor they were certain he would still be alive today. Remy is another one that I miss so much, and again he had been with me for quite some time and was also like part of my family. This story shows the difference of certain West African countries, in Barry's case there was nothing done by the authorities –this was Nigeria. In Remy's case in Abidjan, however, the Ivory Coast authorities did take action.

There was also another tragedy, just before we departed Port Harcourt for dry dock. One of the ABs on leave, a young lad called Sam Bassey who had been with me for almost a year, had drowned in the river close to Eket. There were rumours and speculation surrounding Sam's death but nobody knows for sure what happened.

Another one of my crew whom tragedy struck was Sam Akpa from the local community in Eket, and Sam had been a steward with me for quite some time. Sam would keep my cabin spotless. He would wash and iron my clothes and return them to me in a couple of hours. Sam and I got on really well, I think a couple of the crew thought Sam was too close to me and resented the fact.

Just before Christmas one year, Sam came back on board with a large flat package. I did not know what the package contained nor did I ask, but when the Nigerian crew members were flying to the platform they had to go through the Exxon Mobil security checks before joining the *St Patrick* vessel, so I knew the package was safe.

Captain Bob, my back to back, took turns doing Christmas and new year on board, one year I would do both on board, and the following year Bob would do both on board. This year was my turn and there would be barbecues for both Christmas and New Year. Exxon Mobil always tried to give us a half day for Christmas Day and New Year's Day. This year was no exception. We did our morning work and stopped at 12.30pm. I took the vessel to an anchorage where there was a mobile phone network so as the crew could get a phone call home to wish their families a Merry Christmas. It was a typically sweltering day. The barbecue was arranged for 3pm giving the crew time to bathe and get ready. The Barbie was cranked up with charcoal, and the tables and chairs were set up at the large area at the back of the wheelhouse. The catering crew worked hard all morning to get everything ready. We had party hats, streamers and Christmas decorations to add to the festive feel. At 3pm, I announced on the PA that the barbecue was ready. At the back of the bridge there was a stereo system set up so music could be played during the meal. There was also a microphone set up for the speeches. I was the first one to give a speech. I wished everyone on board a very Merry Christmas and to pass on the same to their families. The Exxon Mobil representative also did the same. Then one of the deck crew said a prayer and we all tucked in to salads, chicken, burgers and spare ribs. The catering crew always did us proud and there was a mixture of continental and national food. Tthe spread was excellent and well received. Everyone congratulated the catering team for their efforts. Just as the camp boss was removing the tin foil and covers from the dishes of food,the Exxon Mobil rep announced that Sam Akpa would like to make a presentation to Captain Alex, the Master on board, Sam stepped forward with a beaming grin, and he was holding the large flat package that I saw him bring on board. He was aware of my passion for football and that I followed Manchester United, who at the time were being coached by the former Aberdeen manager Sir Alex Ferguson.

Sam removed the Christmas wrappings with a flourish and handed me this large hand-made plaque. It was a Manchester United poster that Sam had a friend of his embellish back in Eket. It read: 'Manchester United: The Red Devils. To Captain Alexander Westland'. It was beautiful and I loved it. I could not hide my delight and thanked Sam, shaking his hand and embracing him. I sensed his real pride and pleasure. This was the very first and only time that any of the crew had given me a present. It was a moment that meant so much to me. As the sun went down on an unusual Christmas at sea, I felt a very real sense of closeness between the Nigerians and expats on board. Sam went on leave in the first week of January after the New Year's party with the rest of the Nigerian crew. About five days after the crew change, one of Sam's friends from the same village came to the wheelhouse.

"Sir, I have bad news for you."

"What is it?"

"Sam Akpa has been involved in a motor accident and was killed instantly."

I could not believe this news. I was in shock. The whole crew started streaming up to the bridge, saying that they could not believe the news either. The rest of that day the whole crew were solemn and very quiet.

The Nigerians used to have two church services on board every week: one on a Sunday and the other on a Wednesday. There were certain members of the crew that were nominated as pastors. That evening there was a service arranged in the crew's mess for Sam. I attended the service where they sang hymns and said prayers for Sam and his family. It was deeply sad and very different to a normal church service in Scotland. It lasted about two hours. We arranged a collection for Sam which was sent home to his family on the next crew change. Sam was sadly missed by all, especially by me. This was indicative of how the Nigerians thought, and changed their attitude on a daily basis. They would give you the impression one day that life meant nothing, but when one of the crew died they would have services for them, and then the next day they would be laughing and joking as if nothing had happened. They were very difficult to work out at times.

Although the St Patrick was a workhorse of a vessel she still had to be looked after to ensure she could keep earning her keep. In June 2010, it was in dry dock for its five-year survey. We were booked into a dock at Abidjan on the Ivory Coast and all her ABS classification certificates renewed. This included a hull survey with any damaged steel plates to be removed and replaced. It should have been a straightforward dry dock, but there was an added bonus; after our trial period with Exxon

Mobil, the company had landed a major tender from the same company – the *St Patrick* had obviously impressed. On the back of this excellent news, Chris Woolley and PW Resources decided to upgrade and refit the vessel to DP2. This meant replacing the four engines and installing more powerful MAN engines, new propulsion thrusters, power generators and a Kongsberg K-Pos system, which was the latest type of DP. This was going to cost a stack of money but the *St Patrick* would be a far better vessel. My cabin and the crew accommodation, which was rather tired, were also getting a facelift. In all, a significant investment and commitment by PW Resources.

We sailed from Nigeria for the Carena shipyard in Abidjan. With the extra work, we expected to be in dry dock for around about 4 months. Captain Bob and I were still to continue working eight weeks on and eight weeks off when we went to Abidjan, although we had minimum crewing levels. Apart from essential personnel, most of the crew were sent home. There was going to be a large team working on the vessel in dry dock and my Australian friend Paul was going to be the superintendent. Electricians and mechanical engineering specialists were flown in from the UK. Electricians were employed to strip out all the old electrical systems, run in new cables for all the new machinery, and install the new DP system and generators. The mechanical specialists were employed to work with the chief engineer in installing and testing the new engines. The first setback was the delay in the new engines and the new DP system arriving, which was three months overdue on delivery. In the early weeks, Abidjan was quiet and enjoyable. We used to head to the local bush bars outside the dry dock without any problems. While the poverty in Abidjan was bad it was not as dire as that in Nigeria and Ghana. There was a marked improvement in the houses and the town was much tidier and the roads were certainly a lot cleaner. Abidjan was mostly run by the French until the nation was given its independence in

1960. It was a relatively prosperous African nation, producing cocoa and coffee, and there was still a strong French military presence. As a French-speaking former colony the Ivory Coast was a tranquil place to be for those first few months in dry dock. We went shopping to the malls in the city centre of Abidjan and we never had a problem. Six months were up before we knew it. The rewiring and the prep work for the engines took longer than anticipated. Meanwhile we became interested in the national political situation, and we heard that trouble was brewing. It started in the run-up to the presidential elections in November 2010. President Laurent Gbagbo, who had been in power for many years –although he was nearly ousted by a previous rebel coup –was not popular in many parts of the Ivory Coast. His opponent, Alassane Ouattara, was from the North and he had been gaining ground. A growing number of Ivorians were rooting for this man, a Muslim, to get into office. However, everybody we spoke to said that it was a foregone conclusion that the sitting president would win the election, after all it was really a dictatorship. In the run up to the election, Abidjan was alive with activity and there were canvassers everywhere from both parties, the Ouattara's RDR and Gbagbo's FPI. The rallies were colourful and noisy but peaceful most of the time. Over time they began to get rowdier and our shipping agent advised us to stay close to the shipyard. If we did go out for a beer we should stay near the bush bars outside the shipyard.

On voting day, the shipyard closed all its heavy gates and all the vessels' crews were advised to stay in the ship yard. The next day, 2nd December, the news came through that Ouattara had won the election with 54% of the vote. However, it was declared invalid by the President, and this inflamed the RDR supporters. We heard there was trouble in town as both parties began fighting with each other. People burned houses, shops and cars, and homes were even set alight. The government claimed there was a mistake in the vote counting and that some regions had not been included in the count. To keep the peace, the government announced that there would be a recount. Life quietened down for a spell but there were still reports of fighting between the two parties, especially to the North of the country where the new elected president came from. Everybody in Abidjan became very concerned and it was incredibly tense due to the delay in recounting the votes. As the weeks passed the people of the Ivory Coast were becoming more agitated. You could sense the unrest in the city and we avoided going to the city centre as the skirmishes escalated. Some oil companies were getting their workers out of Abidjan and vessels that were able to leave were told to leave the port. The *St Patrick* still wasn't ready to sail and PW were keeping an eye on the situation. Paul Partridge and I thought we were not in any immediate danger and we kept pushing to get the work done as swiftly as possible.

Then all hell broke loose. It was announced that the President had lost the election and that Ouattara was the winner. But Gbagbo did not accept this decision and was not going to stand down. His party and his supporters were backing him because they had been in power as far back as anyone could remember. The new man, his party and his supporters claimed they had the right to be the new government. This was a big problem because Gbagbo was in charge of the army and he ordered his soldiers to chase the other party from Abidjan. Bitter fighting began, pushing the country into a civil war, with Ouattara's forces forcing their way into the capital. We knew it was not safe. It was time to go. PW booked our flights whilst we could still get out of the country. It was no easy task, however, getting flights in the middle of a mass exodus. The shipyard shut up shop and set up an emergency evacuation plan for their workers and all other personnel in the ship yard should the situation arise. French naval vessels were also standing by to take everybody in the yard out by boat if needed.

As I was driven to the airport with security guards there were gun shots and several massive explosions and brilliant flashes of light as mortars landed close to the motorway. The scene at the airport was crowded, noisy and chaotic, but I managed to get a flight back to Europe, and home eventually to Aberdeen. This left the *St Patrick* unattended. This was a deep concern for everyone, but lives were more important. Paul travelled to Ghana soon after I left, and was one of the last expats to leave Abidjan.

After we left we kept a close eye on the news although there was hardly anything in the local Scottish newspapers or on the local television news. We were following the story on the internet through the African news networks. As the situation became more precarious other countries stepped in to try to get the dictator to stand down and give the new guy his rightful place as president of the Ivory Coast. After months of fighting and killings in this civil war, someone finally managed to persuade the army that they had to support the new president. The dictator was arrested and held prisoner in a big house just outside Abidjan. Some of his followers were never going to accept this decision and continued to fight. The army stepped in and began savagely killing those protesters before life eventually started to quieten down.

In the early spring of 2011, PW were informed that the killings had stopped and that the shipyard had been reopened for business. The vessel's agents said they were back in business and that it was now safe to return. Paul and I were booked on flights back to Abidjan. When I returned we heard harrowing stories of atrocities and saw horrifying pictures of people being burned alive during the conflict. The images of burning people made me sick to the stomach. I wondered how the rest of the world felt about this, as it had been well documented by the media. The port's security guards had done their best but locals from the nearby villages had evacuated their homes. Some had made their way up the river banks and had taken refuge on the *St Patrick*. The guards did not want to turn these people away and allowed them to stay under supervision. It was our job to convince them to return home, and reclaim our vessel. The electricians returned and we managed to finish all the work. Captain Bob, myself and the company agreed we would both be on board for the tests on the new engines, and the new DP system and generators. We both wanted to be certain everything was in excellent working order so we both went on the sea trials. The run back to Nigeria would be a perfect test with the two masters sharing the duties. The company would send a chief officer after a couple of weeks working for Exxon Mobil, I would go on leave and Bob would do an extra six weeks on board. I would then return and Bob would have his eight weeks leave as usual. As the engines could only be run alongside the jetty without the clutches we had to get the Carina tug boats to take us to the open bay where we were secured to a marker buoy. We ran the engines with clutches in and the engineering expert from Germany adjusted all his settings. We then ran up and down the bay a few times while more refinements were made. Everything seemed to be fine. The DP trials were done at sea with Noble Denton from Aberdeen. Their two technicians gave us manual DP so as we could take the vessel down the river and proceed to sea. This meant we could steer the vessel and control the engines with the use of the joystick on the new DP system. It was like sailing a brand new craft. Providing everything was in proper working order at the end of all tests, the vessel would be issued with a FMEA (Failure Mode and Effect Analysis) Certificate, required by all DP 2-3 vessels. When everything was completed and everybody was happy we returned to the Carena yard. The vessel was ready to go – however our FMEA approval hadn't come back. Little did we know that it was not going to be that easy; we thought this would be a sure thing.

It was now 2012, two years after entering the port of

Abidjan. The whole project had taken a lot longer than anticipated and the bills had mounted up. The company was even charged for docking fees during the civil war. The truth was the company did not have enough money to pay the bills and had to borrow money from a competitor in exchange for part of the contract with Exxon Mobil. We were waiting for the all-clear to sail. Bob and I made the vessel secure for sailing and we had a lot of cargo on deck, such as the old engines. All the equipment on deck had to be tack welded down to the deck to make it seaworthy. We did quite a lot of tidying and sprucing up the accommodation so the vessel would look good when we arrived back in Nigeria. When we finally received the all-clear to sail, we departed Abidjan; we had a minimum crew on board for the journey. Bob and I took charge of the bridge watches, Bob was on duty from 6am to 12pm and then 6pm to midnight, and I was on duty from midnight to 6am and from 12pm to 6pm. It was quite strange for both of us as we had always been back-to-back and had never sailed together. We both enjoyed working together and said we would have to do it again sometime. The crew found it strange too as this was the first time that they had both masters on board at the same time. Some of them would joke asking who was in charge but most conceded I was the boss because I was the longest-serving master. Both of us had a watch keeper on with us as the waters were busy between the Ivory Coast and Nigeria. So we were always alert and monitored the radios constantly. We made sure that we were always some miles off the land so as to avoid any onshore pirates. The journey went well with no major incidents and the chief engineer was keeping a close watch on the new engine temperatures. When we arrived back from dry dock in 2012, we went straight to the Idoho West anchorage. The plan was for Exxon Mobil to come offshore with a team of auditors, if all went well then we would get our full crew on board ready for work this would include a full team of divers and a dive spread. PW were still going to be running the vessel but now the Broron Group, a Nigerian oil and gas business based in Lagos, who lent PW the money, were going to be running the contract with Exxon Mobil. This was strange for me, Bob and the PW crew as we had always worked directly with Exxon Mobil up until then. The *St Patrick* was to be chartered to Broron. We sat at the anchorage for a few days before the Broron personnel transferred from other vessels in the oilfield started to come on board. This was a difficult period, there were clashes between the Broron and the PW guys arguing over cabins and perks. The PW crew had been on board for some time and had bagged the new accommodation because they were permanent crew. But the Broron personnel wanted the new accommodation and even tried to throw some of the PW crew and their belongings out of their cabins. Bob and I had to step in as peacemakers. It is not easy being master of the vessel in this situation. We had never seen this kind of acrimony before. We had always believed that the vessel crews were like a family and tried to get on as best as they could, but not in Nigeria.

When the audit team came from Exxon Mobil they were delighted with the vessel, new engines, new DP system and the other work that had been carried out. The only problem was the certificates we were waiting for from ABS, the vessel's class authority, had not arrived. Bob and I explained to the Exxon audit team that all the paperwork was coming and hoped Exxon Mobil would allow us to work until all the paperwork was in order. The Broron representative asked if we knew how long the paperwork would take to come but while we had done everything we could, we didn't know the answer. Chris had been chasing ABS and the flag state several times but without much success. Exxon gave us extra time to get the paperwork sorted but insisted that it all had to be in place before they would allow us to start work. Chris was deeply frustrated as he had worked hard on getting us out of dry dock. Time was money. Now ABS was holding us up, when we needed to start working. Yet there seemed to be no urgency with ABS. The paperwork took a couple of weeks to come through then Exxon came back and agreed to sign the contract. We were back on hire. It was then that we started crewing up until we were at a full complement. I stayed on board for a couple of weeks and then went on leave. At last, the *St Patrick* was back to work in Nigeria.

# 11

# HEARING THE SHOCKING NEWS AT HOME

Thousands of miles away from my hut, Helen was having a day off from work. She was at home in Montrose getting ready to go shopping with her friend June. It was about noon on Tuesday 14th May 2013, and she was listening to Radio 2 as she cleared up her lunchtime dishes, before heading out to our holiday home in a caravan park, 12 miles away on the outskirts of Arbroath.

Montrose is a historic, medium-sized Scottish town, about halfway between the two cities of Aberdeen and Dundee. It is at the mouth of the River South Esk beside the Montrose Basin – a wonderful sheltered habitat for sea birds, especially geese, and other wildlife. The port is small but it has been able to operate successfully, servicing the oil and gas industry in the North Sea. One of the main employers in the area is the pharmaceutical giant GlaxoSmithKline which has a major plant making drugs for the treatment of respiratory diseases and HIV and AIDS. Helen and I moved back to Montrose after our spell in Spain. She had found work in a local supermarket and was near her friends and family, which was better for her while I was working in West Africa. It's a close-knit town popular with summer visitors and while it has social issues like most other Scottish towns it is a decent place to live.

In 1996 we had moved to Spain because Steven, our son lived there. We had visited him a few times and then decided to move there permanently. We were there for ten years in total, but our grandchildren were living in Scotland and we missed seeing them grow up. So we came back to Britain, and rented a house in Ferryden, Montrose, close to the harbour. It was a handy location for us both, as Helen's line dancing was around the corner and there was a lot of local fishing for me. June had been on the phone and was awaiting Helen's arrival at the holiday home when Helen heard a knock at the front door. When she answered, a well-dressed man and woman were standing on the path.

"Hello. Are you Mrs Helen Westland?"

"Yes," Helen replied.

"We're members of the Scottish Police Service. We do not wish to alarm you, but we have some bad news for you."

Helen invited them in to the house. Her mind was racing and she knew something serious had happened to me or someone else in the family. She sat down in the lounge on the settee as the officers proceeded to tell Helen the shocking news.

"Your husband's vessel was attacked by Nigerian pirates. As far as we know, your husband, Alexander "Joe" Westland, has been taken hostage. We think he is being held somewhere in the jungle. Nobody knows for sure where he is being held at the moment," said the policewoman.

"Oh my God. What on earth," said Helen, as she held her hand up to her mouth

She could hear the police explaining what was happening and she knew I was in grave danger.

"Chris, his managing director, is aware of the situation and standing by with an emergency team for phone calls from the kidnappers. Chris told us to tell you that everything will be OK and that you have to stay strong. He will call you later," said the policewoman.

She added that the British government were also aware of the situation. Helen tried to process all this incredible information.

She wanted to tell her family and June, her best friend. But the police were firm; Helen must not tell anyone because it may affect the negotiations between Chris and the kidnappers and could put my life in danger. She had to keep this terrible news to herself for now. She wondered how she was supposed to cope with this on her own.

Helen is a sensible woman who is emotionally strong and, she won't mind me saying, stubborn. She convinced the police officers that she had to tell June as they were supposed to be going shopping together. So the two police officers agreed and escorted Helen to the holiday home. June was let in on the bad news and she and Helen hugged. June could not take in what she was being told. June and I have known each other for a very long time, so the news was a shock to her. She was advised not to tell another soul – and she promised not to say a word.

The police drove Helen back to Montrose. They wanted to be on standby in case the kidnappers called her. The police suggested that it would be best if they stayed with her until the ordeal was over, if she agreed of course. With only one bedroom in our house it was going to be a bit cramped, but they would all manage. The sitting room has spacious settees and loungers and the police officers said they could sleep there. The police worked in shifts: two on each 12 hour shift with 24 hours a day support – for as long as it was going to take. If she went out, the police would escort her. They knew that the kidnappers had my phones and there was every chance they might try and phone her to gain more emotional leverage. Helen was briefed on how to react on the phone, and what to say if the kidnappers called. The police also attached a recording device to her phone so they could listen in on anything that was said. For Helen, the waiting was terrible. With no news or contact from the kidnappers, the mood was very grim indeed. These were desperate times but secrecy was necessary. Nevertheless, Helen felt guilty about not telling the family, especially our daughter and grandchildren who live only nine miles away in neighbouring Brechin. We see a lot of Tracey and the grandchildren, David, Dean and Darcie, and Helen spends time with them nearly every day when I am away. No doubt they would start to wonder why Granny had not been in to see them if this went on for several days. However, Helen was worried about how they'd react when they did find out. If I was killed she felt they would never forgive her for keeping quiet. But the officers assured her it was the right thing to do. They could not risk anything leaking out on Facebook or through social media, as a result of the grandchildren possibly telling some of their friends. In the officers' eyes this could have made my predicament more dangerous and the kidnappers would also be able to phone and threaten my family.

Helen was provided with and shown how to operate a voice recorder which she had to carry with her at all times in case the pirates did call her. She had to make sure as soon as the phone rang that if she did not recognise the number the recorder was switched on. On the second day, just after lunch, Helen received a call from Chris. He asked how she was doing and again told her to stay strong. Chris told Helen that the pirates had called and that I was indeed being kept in the jungle. He also told her that she could be sure he was doing his very best to get me out of there safely and as quickly as possible. He told Helen that he had talked to me and that I sent my love and wanted her to be strong and that I would see her when this nightmare was over. Helen did not know what to think or do, she was in a daze, and she tried to imagine what I was going through and how I was handling this terrible situation. Helen's mind was in turmoil throughout this period. What would she do if anything happened to me and I did not return home? It did not bear thinking about. June was to be her rock for the next few days and her shoulder to cry on, and this was turning into a nightmare for both of us.

Helen lived hand in hand with the police until the day after my release. During this time, Helen also worried about what the neighbours were thinking – all these strange cars parked on the road and strange people coming to the door. But to the neighbours' credit none of them approached Helen or asked what was going on when they met Helen on the street. They must have known something was going on but thought better about getting involved. They all went about their business and didn't ask any questions. It was also a case of the police being nice and discreet about how and when they entered the house, and were very careful not to park too close to our house when they could avoid it.

# 12

# THE PIRATES' OPENING GAMBITS

My face was puffed up with bites. My fingers, forearms and feet were now red raw with rashes and sores, while my stomach was knotted with cramping pains. It had rained throughout the night, a lashing tropical torrent which made the whole forest smell fresh like a shampoo factory. The water dripped through the roof onto my neck and head and made me shiver. Then, as a steamy cauldron of heat began to boil up on Wednesday, my second day of captivity, the elder brother, as he was called, stepped into the hut. He had on a pair of my tracksuit bottoms and a black T-shirt that I did not recognise, and a pair of sandals with no socks. He had his cigarettes and lighter in his hand.

"How are you doing?" he inquired.

"I feel bad. The heat is terrible for me. And the ants and the mosquitoes are too much to bear. I want to go home," I said squatting on the wooden plank.

"You will go home after we speak to your boss on the phone."

I was delirious with the clammy heat and I told him that I had been promised an electric fan.

"Don't worry. One of the boats has gone to the village to get a generator, a fan and a light bulb. Things will get better," he assured me.

I told him that I was getting stomach cramps and was not feeling too good. I had nothing to eat. He nodded and said he would try to get me some chicken and rice later that day. An hour later, Nick and Thomas came in to the hut. I was relieved they weren't carrying their machine guns this time. They asked the same questions as the elder brother and I repeated my condition.

"Be strong, Captain. We will get you a fan to cool you down," said Nick.

They also told me that they would make the first call to my office just after lunchtime.

"The company will get a call from us. They will pay what we want and after that you will be back with your family," he explained.

I did not know whether to believe him or not. I tried to make out by the tone of his voice if he was being serious. I wanted to believe him. They asked which number they should call. I showed them Chris's number in Lagos. They asked about the overseas numbers. I lied and told them I did not have it. The only number I was willing to show them was Chris's. I knew he could handle the situation. The overseas number was under the name of the accountant in PW overseas, so there was no way of them knowing where on my phone to find the number. Later that morning, the elder brother kept his word. One of the boats arrived with a generator and a fan, although it wasn't very powerful against the intensifying heat, it was better than nothing. When he got the fan working, they pointed it directly at my face – it was sheer luxury. The elder brother did all the wiring himself, it looked like he knew what he was doing. After he got the fan going he asked me if that was better. I told him that it was a lot better and thanked him.

By now I was getting sharper pains in my stomach, and needed to go the toilet regularly. The guards watched me slide down an earthy bank, wet from the night's rain, to a boggy cesspit where I crouched and held onto a bush. Without toilet paper this was an increasingly unpleasant experience. The diarrhoea was bad, the water was running from me and there was nowhere to wash my hands or keep myself properly clean. The mosquito bites were becoming fiercer and I began to worry about catching malaria. I had had malaria before and it is not nice at all.

Back in the hut, I could see the pirates eating lunch and drinking more of the local hooch. The smell of their lunch cooking was making me feel nauseous. They were cooking fish in spices and eating them whole, to me the smell was unbearable. I knew from the cooks on the *Saint Patrick* that this dish was called pepper soup, and is normally eaten with yams and French bread.

Unarmed, Nick and Thomas returned to the hut.

"We're going to call your boss now. What's his name?"

"He's called Chris," I replied, keen to be as helpful as possible.

They said I had to go outside with them and that they would give me an ear piece. They helped me walk across the clearing scattered with pine needles and litter. There were ants and other, unusual insects crawling everywhere. This was made all the more unpleasant as I was still in my bare feet – the socks they had given me were now ruined and had begun to smell, so I had discarded them. Tropical birds chirped away happily in the trees. I had to dodge the tree stumps that the pirates were using for seats and tables. Nick had one ear piece and I had the other one. It was then that I found out what the string hanging from the trees was for; the mobile phone was attached to it, to get a better signal. Nick dialled the number and then hauled the phone above his head with the string.

*Click, click, click, click. Ring. Ring. Ring.*

"Hullo. Who is this calling?" said Chris on the end of the line.

"Hi, are you Chris?" said Nick.

"Yes. I am," came the reply.

"Listen carefully, Chris. I am going to put your captain on the line," said Nick, and he nodded at me to speak.

110

"Hello, Chris. It's me, Alex. I'm being held by Nigerian pirates. I was taken off the *St Patrick* at gunpoint. These guys want to talk to you."

Nick interrupted our conversation, pointing at me.

"Right, Chris. You heard the captain. We've got some business to do," he said.

"I want to know that my captain is safe and unharmed. Let me speak to him again," insisted Chris.

"He is safe and well looked after. We need to speak about business."

"Put my captain back on," said Chris

I could see that Nick was desperate to get on with the business, but he let me talk again.

"Chris, I'm being held hostage and the pirates want money for my release."

"I know, mate. How are you doing?"

"Not good. I've been badly bitten and the heat's killing me. I've got terrible diarrhoea."

"Are you being well treated and have they physically abused you in any way?"

"No. There's been no physical abuse, only heavy threats. I've had water but nothing to eat."

Chris knew that I took medication for my bad back and other ailments.

"Do you have your prescription drugs?"

"No. I don't have them."

Nick took control again and asked Chris what was going on. Chris said I was quite an old man and not very well. He explained I had collapsed the last time I was at home and I needed my prescription drugs or I would be in serious trouble.

"I'm going to send you a text message with the list of drugs that the Captain requires."

"Look, Chris. If you want the captain back you need to pay us 150 Million Naira for his release," Nick said.

"Come on! There is no way we have this kind of money, PW Resources isn't a big oil company. We're a small firm and we can't get that sort of money. You are being totally, unreasonable." Chris talked to Nick in a very calm voice. I was kind of expecting this reply from Chris, I knew he would not have this amount of cash. My heart sank, I was obviously hoping that he would be able to get the money. In my mind, if he had at least said that he could get the money, even though he couldn't, the pirates would at least give him some time and this would maybe save my life. But because Chris said immediately that he could not get the amount of money that they wanted, I thought I was in serious trouble. I now expected them to do something bad to me to force Chris's hand.

"How much can you give then… to save your Captain's life?"

"Well, the most I have at the moment is 7 million Naira,"

Nick burst out laughing. But I could see that underneath he was angry and shocked by what Chris had told him. I wondered if 7 million Naira was all I was worth. I fully expected Chris to tell them that he had more than 7 million Naira. I thought, *Oh my God I am dead*. 150 million Naira was worth £528,434, whilst 7 million Naira was only worth £24,660. I understood why Nick and Thomas laughed and thought the offer from Chris was a joke, and I also understood when Nick told me that he was not at all happy and that Chris was playing with my life.

"Chris, I thought the captain was your friend? You cannot like him very much, just to offer this small amount of money. This sum will not save your captain's life," Nick said.

Chris remained calm and said he would need time to try to find more cash. He asked Nick to call him back at six that evening.

"OK, Chris. You go and speak to your people. But I warn you, you will have to do a lot better. Is that clear?"

"Very clear. Now let me speak to the Captain again."

I was very nervous now. The phone call was nearly over and

nothing was agreed. In fact, both sides seemed poles apart, and my life was hanging in the balance.

"Chris, please help me. Do your best. I do not know how much more of this I can stand," I begged.

"Alex, we are doing our best. We will have you out of there soon. I promise you, they will not hurt you," he tried to assure me.

I really wanted to believe Chris but I knew it was not that simple.

"I'm going to go and see how much money I can raise. Goodbye Alex, be strong and I will speak to you tonight."

"Does Helen know?" I blurted out almost in tears.

"Yes, she is aware and she is bearing up. Helen passes on her love and wants you to stay strong."

The call was over. Nick and Thomas asked me if Chris and I were really best friends. Nick asked if I understood how little 7 million Naira was. I told him that I did understand but told him that Chris was only paid the Naira part of the contract and that the dollar part of the contract was sent overseas. It was similar to the vessel not being allowed to carry dollars on board. Chris was not allowed to keep dollars in Nigeria. It was only the Naira payments that Chris had to work with to pay all the salaries and provisions for the local boats and crews. So I wasn't too surprised when Chris told Nick that he did not have 150 Million Naira. Nick did not believe what I told him, he said that Chris would have to get the money if he wanted to save my life.

I was escorted back to the hut, and again I had to walk through all the pine needles, insects and trash. The walk back seemed to take ages. I could not stop thinking about the conversation between Chris and Nick. Was Chris going to manage to come up with the money that these guys wanted to save my life? I was then left in isolation in my jungle hut to mull over my fate. I'm not a person who cries easily, but I was gently sobbing as I thought about Helen and her torment at home thousands of miles away. After the first phone call – the opening gambit in the chess game for my life – I was shut back in my prison. I felt wretched, I was not going to get out of here alive. I knew that PW had been toiling financially because of the delays and extra costs in the dry dock. Chris could not simply conjure up the kind of money the pirates were demanding. I felt lost and lonely. My moment of solace was pulling out a cigarette and savouring a few puffs.

Why was I not getting any food? I was asked if I could eat Nigerian food but that would make me worse. It is a rough stew made from grisly meat of often dubious origin. I knew from the *St Patrick* that local food was often no more than scraps of meat and bones. The smell of it was enough to make me feel sick. All day it was intensely hot and humid and my condition was worsening. I needed the toilet even more frequently, and climbing down the bank into the bog was becoming more difficult. My trousers were soiled with muck and mud from the bank and my T-shirt was wringing with sweat. I was beginning to stink. For a man who would normally shower twice a day on the vessel and change my clothes every day, this compounded my discomfort.

It was later in the afternoon when Thomas came back into the hut.

"Here, Captain. Some more bottles of water for you," he said.

"Have you received a text from Chris about my prescription drugs?" I asked.

"Yes, I did. We are seeing a doctor to get your drugs. It's a big list and I'm not sure if we can get them all here in Nigeria."

"But I need these drugs."

"Be strong. We will do our best."

He walked off. *Be strong!* All I could think about was the aggressive teenage pirate who told me if my company did not pay he would gleefully set me on fire and burn me alive. My thoughts turned again to Helen in Montrose and my family back in Scotland. What would they do if I did not come home?

How would Helen cope? While Helen is a very strong person nothing prepares you for this kind of tragic event. What was I to do? Although I do not go to church often I wanted to believe that there was a God in Heaven who might show mercy on me. I began praying that he would help me. *Please God help me.*

At 6pm that evening, Nick and Thomas returned to the hut. They were armed again, this time brandishing their AK-47 machine-guns in a more menacing way. I could tell they had been drinking or smoking the local weed. An electric shiver of fear conducted right down my spine. For a moment, I thought this might be my end. They're going to kill me. But then rational thinking kicked in: surely they wouldn't kill me now, I was a bargaining chip. They needed me alive.

"Be strong, Captain. We're going to speak to your boss again," said Nick.

"Let's hope he's been successful," interrupted Thomas.

"If your boss is sensible and gives us what we want, then you will soon be back home with your beautiful family."

Nick told me to follow him outside. They were going to make the call and I was told not to speak unless they nodded. Again we went over to where my mobile phone was hanging from a branch. Nick pulled it down and punched in the number.

*Click, click, click, click. Ring. Ring and Ring.*

"Hello," Chris said.

"Hello, Chris. Have you got the money for us?"

"Let me speak to the captain first."

Nick motioned to me to speak.

"Hi, Chris. It's me."

"Are you being well treated, have you had some food yet, Alex?"

"I've had water but no food. I'm really not well."

"Hang in there, Alex. Helen says hello. We're all working on your release."

"Did you manage to get the money we wanted?" interrupted Nick.

"Yes, I've managed to find a little bit more than I offered in the morning," replied Chris.

"How much?"

"I now have nine million Naira."

We want 150 million Naira, do you really want your Captain back, it does not look like it to us. Thomas butted in and said, "Chris you have to be serious."

As the call went on, more of the pirates began to gather around Nick, sensing his anger. They were all becoming irate as Thomas clicked the safety catch of his machine-gun off and on.

"Chris, you are playing with this man's life," Nick said again.

"What you are offering will not save him! You have to take us seriously. We are not playing here. You will have to do better or suffer the consequences," he bellowed down the phone, as the others pressed forward.

"Look, I've told you we are a small company. We are trying our very best."

"Borrow the money from others or Exxon Mobil!" shouted Nick.

"It does not work like that," replied Chris.

"Don't tell us how it doesn't work! Your captain is in danger. Remember this," Nick snapped.

"Give me some more time. I will call you tomorrow morning. Have you got the drugs for the Captain?"

"We are working on it," replied Nick as he began to calm down.

"You must get the Captain his drugs. This is very important. If you don't, you will have a very sick man on your hands."

Chris asked to talk to me again and Nick nodded for me to go ahead.

"Please keep going, Alex. We're doing our best to find more

money. You understand that we can't get the kind of money that Nick wants."

"Please Chris, do your best. I'm scared out of my wits here. I do not know how much longer I can last in these conditions," I whimpered.

"Everything will be all right, we will have you out of there soon. I promise."

Throughout this exchange, with Chris on the back foot over money and Nick getting angrier, I felt absolutely helpless. I was like a goat being traded by two sides that were miles apart. The call came to an abrupt end and I was despondent. There had been no agreement or resolution. It is unfair for me to say now, but I was angry with Chris at the time for not getting more money. How much was my life really worth? The pirates headed back over to their open fire and their camp cooking. I was marched back into the hut as the daylight began to fade quickly on the clearing. The mosquitoes were biting and my joints were stiff and in agony. How and when was my nightmare going to end?

# 13

## MY HEALTH IN THE JUNGLE WORSENS

Night fell again in the jungle. There was a brief tropical downpour which drenched everything out in the open and dripped through the roof of the hut. The foetid aroma of the glistening palm leaves and sopping bushes was heavy in the air. After the rain, the now familiar shrieking, cooing and squawking of birds was joined by the click-click, click-clack of insects and the buzzing of flies. My diarrhoea was unabated and messy. I called the guards many times so I could venture down the slimy slope to the boggy marsh.

As a sea captain, I have always been trained to examine the options of any given situation. In truth, I thought Chris would not be able to come up with the money the pirates were demanding. That was the reality, wasn't it? The kidnappers wanted 150 million Naira – a hell of lot of money. I was not sure how much less they would settle for, if they would settle for any less at all. I began to think of ways of killing myself. Maybe grabbing a gun and turning it on myself would be an option? However, I've never even handled a machine-gun, so how could I be sure that it would work. No, this was a mad thought as the guns were never out of the pirates' hands. Maybe I could jump into the water when I was out on a toilet break? If I did not drown, maybe the alligators would get me? In my mind this was better than getting burnt alive. No, this would never work either.

I was now so ill and exhausted I could see that even the pirates were getting concerned about my health. Then I had a better idea: make my illness look a lot worse than it actually was. As Chris had planted the seed regarding my health not being good and all the medication I had to take, I decided that acting very sick might work. After all, I had to do something to get out of here. If nothing was concluded by Friday I could be here the whole weekend. That was a terrifying thought. I did not think I would survive that long.

It was dark in the hut and now almost midnight. The camp fire had died down and some of the pirates had gone to bed in the larger part of the hut next door. One of the younger guards was sitting on a wooden stump a few yards away, he was nearly asleep.

"Hey! I need the toilet. Help me out!" I called over to him.

He woke up and trained his gun on me. One of his fellow pirates sitting nearby stirred and approached.

"What's up, Captain?" he asked.

"Let me out for the toilet."

They both came over and I started to stagger, stumbling onto the ground.

"Help me. Help me. I need the toilet," I said.

The two guards grabbed me and gave me support. I made them help me down into the boggy marsh. I lent on them heavily and made them support me all the way back to the hut and back onto my wooden bed. I repeated this a few more times during the night, each time making my condition seem worse. I was lying on the wooden bed and pretended to make an attempt to get off the bed for a drink of water. I fell to the ground hard and lay there. The wood went up in the air and fell to the ground with a bang. The two ran to me and put the wood back on the staging and then helped me to lie down again.

Back in Montrose, they had heard about the first phone calls. Helen was deeply unhappy about keeping the news of my kidnapping from Tracey, our daughter. After the third day, she made a brave decision and told the police that she had to go to Brechin and tell Tracey. The police officers said they understood, but Helen agreed not to tell our grandchildren at this stage. She knew the police feared something slipping out on Facebook or other social media. On Wednesday afternoon, Helen drove to Brechin to break the devastating news. She was not looking forward to the reaction. Our eldest grandson, David, who was 21, was there but thankfully the younger two, Dean and Darcie, were out. David is a sensible and trustworthy guy and Helen knew he would do his best to help our family. So when Helen sat down with Tracey, David was let in on the situation too. David was asked to ensure the younger grandchildren had indeed gone out. She then proceeded to tell them all she knew about my situation. Helen had sworn them to secrecy and explained to them why the police wanted as few people as possible to know. This was still a hostage situation with the kidnappers capable of using all kinds of leverage to get their way. Even from such a distance away. The authorities in Nigeria and the UK were trying to keep a lid on an international news story breaking out. For them, it was imperative that nothing was done that might jeopardise my chances of getting back home alive.

Tracey and David were in absolute shock. They were devastated and could not take in what Helen was telling them. Tracey and David asked a host of questions but Helen simply did not have the answers. The only comfort she could give them was that she had spoken to Chris on the phone. He had assured her that everything was being done by everyone to get me home as soon as they possibly could. Negotiations were ongoing with the kidnappers. Helen assured them that I had not been treated badly. Tracey knew about the dangers of expats working in West Africa and understood there had been a spate of kidnapping going on but she never imagined that her own dad would be a victim. She was devastated and shocked, and feared the worst.

Back in the hut, it was now my third day in captivity and daylight crept through the tree canopy. The two guards had told Nick and Thomas about the night's incidents. They both came in early to see me in the hut.

"How are you doing, Captain?"

"Ahhh, I'm in a lot of pain," I said without moving from my plank.

"You look very pale. I can see that," said Nick.

"Just take it easy if you have to get up," said Thomas, who was looking rather concerned.

"I'm in a lot of pain and feel very weak," I repeated.

They both stepped back outside and I heard them discussing my health in pidgin English.

"It's not good if we end up with a dead man," I overheard one of them say.

I was wondering if I was getting to them with my act. I certainly felt as if my act was having some impact on them, at least they were saying they were worried about my health. Was now the time to take my act a step further?

An hour later, around 7am, I heard my jaunty ring-tone spring into life and knew it was Chris calling as arranged. The two pirates came back into the hut and said I had to speak to Chris. I made out that I was trying to move but I swayed from side to side and buckled at the knees. Nick and Thomas grabbed me and helped me to where the phone was hanging. I made the journey through the pine needles and the trash very difficult for Nick and Thomas; I refused to walk and they had to carry me to the phone, they both took one of my arms and placed them over their shoulders to keep me upright. They were both strong guys and managed to get me to the phone without too much of a problem, all the time they were talking to me and telling me to stay strong.

"Sit down. Sit down," said Nick.

A wooden chair had been brought over from the camp fire,

and I collapsed my body onto it. I had one ear piece and Nick the other.

"How are you bearing up?" Chris asked.

"Badly. I'm not well and in a lot of pain. I'm very weak," I said emphasising the agony in my voice.

"Be strong, Alex. We are doing our utmost best to get you out of there. Have they got your drugs yet?"

"No. I'm very weak," I slurred.

"Put me back onto Nick," said Chris, although he knew Nick was listening.

"Yes, Chris," said Nick.

"What are you doing about the Captain's drugs?"

"We're trying and as soon as we can locate the drugs we will buy them and give them to your Captain," he said. "And what are you doing about our money?" he continued

Chris told him he had been able to get the total to 10.5million Naira. Nick told him he was still playing with my life and he had to get more money. Chris said he was trying his best, but Nick said it was not good enough and he must try much harder.

"Well, I need some more time."

"OK, call us back this evening. But you need to start being serious about the money."

Throughout that day I did everything I could to give the impression that I was getting worse. They could plainly see all the bites and sores that peppered my skin. It wasn't hard to convince them that my health was indeed getting worse. I was starting to believe it myself. I was not well by any stretch of the imagination, having no food was making me weak but I was obviously trying to make things look a lot worse than they were.

It was 6pm when the next phone call came through. I refused to walk, and Nick and Thomas had to carry me out to the phone. I was laying my sickness on really thick now. I refused to walk at all, and when we were halfway from my hut to the phone, Nick had to ask another one of the pirates to help him and Thomas with my flagging body. After a struggle, they managed to get me to the phone, where they sat me down on a chair. I tried to watch their reaction, it seemed like I was convincing them that I was really quite sick. I was now giving the impression that I was very poorly, I even made out that it was difficult for me to speak to Chris. When Nick asked how much money Chris had come up with and Chris told him, Nick shook his head.

"You are really not doing well, Chris. This is still not enough," said Nick

"Look, I might be able to get some more tomorrow. I am trying to get someone tonight who has more money but I can't promise anything. Give me until tomorrow."

"You have until then, then that's it. Or else."

The call ended and I felt bad. Nick had given Chris an ultimatum: find the money or suffer the consequences. Was Chris going to be able to find enough money to keep these guys happy? I doubted this. I was hoping that PW overseas would help Chris with money, but getting cash from Ireland to Nigeria fast would be another problem. I felt that everything was against me.

All that night when I went out to the toilet, I made them carry me – even during a heavy rain storm. My drastic plan was having an impact as the pirates were all chatting in pidgin English about how sick I was. They didn't want their bounty to bow out early.

Early on Friday morning, I needed to show how delirious I was. I did not want to spend the weekend here without any food, medication or comfort. My act had to go a bit further. I knew Nick and Thomas would stay in the hut next door that night. They were worried now about my health. If I died they would be stuck with a dead body and they would get no money. I trembled badly, shivering in my own sweat.

I managed to get my heart racing. I shouted for help

*"Arghh. Arghhh. Ahhhh!"* I groaned as loudly as I could. "Please help me."

The two guards at the door ran towards me and tried to calm me down. Thomas was pulling on his T-shirt when he came in, pushing the two guards out of the way and putting his hand on my forehead. He was shocked to see how hot I was. I took a hold of his hand and put it on the left side of my chest. I gave the impression that it was hard to talk.

"My heart, my heart, I am dying," I gasped.

I could see that Thomas was very scared and he called for Nick.

"Get some more water," he shouted to one of the young guards.

When a large bottle of water was passed to him, Thomas poured it over my head, chest and arms, Nick came running in and Thomas said to him in pidgin English.

"This man is very sick we have to do something," confirmed Thomas.

After looking after me for several minutes and dabbing my head with water, Nick said to Thomas that they would call Chris at 6.30am that morning. Daylight seemed to take an age as I writhed in mock agony. At 6:30, Nick and Thomas carried me out to the hanging phone again.

"I can't do this. I'm dying. Help me. Get me to a doctor. Please. Please," I begged.

"You are not going to die. Please be strong. You will be out of here today."

Had my ploy worked? In my heart and head I did not believe them or trust them. Even if they did get money, I thought, they would just kill me anyway. I just hoped it was going to be a quick bullet and not set on fire. They carried me over to the jungle chair again. This time I could not even sit up straight. I was falling over. Most of the pirates were gathered around watching. Two of them gripped me firmly in the chair to stop me tumbling.

Nick dialled the number, Chris answered within two rings. There was no time for pleasantries.

"Chris, how much money do you have now? Your captain is very sick. He's had a heart attack."

"What? How? Put my captain on immediately? Is he there?" demanded Chris.

"Yes."

"Speak, Captain. Speak to Chris," said Nick, as he pulled the phone nearer so that my voice would be picked up by the tiny microphone attached to the earpiece by a voice cable.

"Hi… Chris," I gasped.

"Alex, how do they know or suspect you had a heart attack?"

"I collapsed and have had severe pains in my chest. I was trembling and my heart was pumping fast," I told him in a gasping voice.

"You be strong. Try and stay calm put Nick on the phone immediately."

"Yes, Chris," Nick said.

"My captain is a very sick man. I told you to get his drugs and you haven't done this. We have to do something soon or you will end up getting nothing. I repeat if anything happens to my captain, you will get nothing. Do you understand?"

"OK. You have until 10am to get as much as you can. We will call you back then."

I had one further chance to speak to Chris. He repeated the familiar mantra "Be strong", and that he would have me out of there later that day. The call was finished and I was returned to the hut. I continued to breathe heavily, almost hyperventilating, and I was drenched in sweat. What if this was too much for the kidnappers? Better to get rid of the evidence and dump the body. Surely this would be easier for them now. I was convinced they would kill me after they got some money. They would do this because they were not getting anywhere near the amount they wanted.

Thomas stayed with me for a long time, pouring the cheap cold water over my head and face: this water came in small plastic bags. The Nigerians drank it but expats were advised to avoid drinking it. Thomas showed a remarkable level of care. Was this even compassion? Surely not?

"Captain Alex, be strong. You are not going to die. Your people will come for you today and you will see a doctor at the hospital tonight."

I did not have a cigarette that day, I was scared it would give the impression that I was all right.

# 14

# A CAPTAIN'S RANSOM

Nick and Thomas carried me to the tree where my phone was hanging. This was a critical call. How would it turn out? Along with my aching guts, there were now butterflies in my stomach. Was there anything I could do or say during this call that would improve this desperate situation that I found myself in? My mind was in turmoil. Nick called Chris and got straight to the point. How much money had he managed to amass? Chris told him the amount.

I've got 13.1 million Naira [£54,000] which I can get to you later today. That's all I could manage and it has not been easy at all.

"OK. Only because the captain is so sick we will accept your offer. If he was not sick you would have had to have found a lot more money. The transfer has to be done today as the captain needs to see a doctor urgently," Nick said.

This comment from Nick surprised me as he seemed to be the hardest of them all. If he was softening, then maybe there was a little hope for me, but was this just words? At least these words gave me a little bit of encouragement at the time.

Chris agreed and said he would have the money together by 1pm. Two Nigerian employees from PW who knew the local area would come to an arranged meeting point. Nick told Chris that he would call back at 1pm and give the driver the instructions.

"No police, no tricks or the Captain dies," said Nick.

What's the driver's mobile phone number?" asked Nick.

"You don't need it. All arrangements will be made through me. Do you understand that?"

"All right. I will be in touch," agreed Nick reluctantly.

After this call there was certainly a sense of restlessness in the camp. I could just make out Nick and Thomas talking to the elder brother. There was plenty of nodding of heads. It looked as if he was giving his approval for the exchange. Several boats arrived with new faces and there was great activity with several of the younger pirates collecting water bottles and belongings. They were basically tidying the place up. I wondered why they were doing this when some of the pirates had told me that they lived there. Could I believe anything they were telling me?

As I continued with my act of being seriously sick, I tried to get inside the pirates' heads. Could I see any sign of pity in any of them? Could I see any signs that some of the pirates were going to ignore the instructions by the so called bosses, take the money and kill us all and run?

The pirates were all so busy now rushing around and planning for the rest of the day that it was very hard to see what any of them were thinking. I just had to pray that their moral conscience would outweigh any evil. It was now blazing hot overhead and stiflingly humid. I was still being bitten but I didn't even feel them now. I had not eaten for four days yet, that was not bothering me. I heard my phone ringing again and assumed it must be 1pm. It was Chris confirming that his guys were ready to leave. Nick gave detailed instructions for the rendezvous. I was dragged out and laid down in a shady spot. I was like an exhausted, empty shell of a human, but my senses remained highly attuned to what was going on.

"Listen carefully," said Nick.

"Your driver must go to the village of Abobo and head down to the harbour. They must take a hire boat – alone with no police – and head out in a southerly direction for three miles. There must be no police. I repeat that. Our boat will meet your guys there and you will get the Captain back, once we have our money."

Back at the PW base, Chris was deeply unhappy with these arrangements. He had to make a judgement about trusting these kidnappers. This meeting in boats was not something he had thought of. He thought the exchange was going to be done onshore. Chris had been in contact with the authorities and with the insurance company, he was taking a massive risk, as it could all go wrong and end up with the deaths of not just me but two more work colleagues. Somehow he felt that Nick was good for his word. In truth, he had no immediate alternative. When I heard this arrangement I began panicking. An exchange in open sea? I had seen what these guys were able and willing to do. They might simply turn their machine guns on me, our two office staff and the boat hire crew, and kill us all.

Whatever my concerns, the arrangement was agreed upon. It would take up to three and a half hours for Alabo and Omini, the two volunteers, to get to the village, plus more time to find a boat to hire. Chris didn't know how easy or difficult that might be. The driver would call Chris when he reached the village and then Chris would contact Nick. They both agreed.

"Let me speak to the Captain now."

Nick nodded to me and I raised myself up with the help of two pirates.

"Hi Chris," I said in the most painful and pathetic voice I could muster.

"Please be strong, mate. Nick and I have agreed a settlement. You will be out of there either late this afternoon or early this evening. I will see you soon."

"I sincerely hope so," I said in a low and painful voice.

After the phone call I feigned another heart attack, and the guys were deeply concerned.

"Hold on, Captain. We will be getting you out of here soon. You will get to see a doctor soon," said Thomas.

This was the first time during all my days of captivity that I began to think there might be a slither of a chance. It was freedom or death, only time would tell.

Thomas poured more water over me.

"Be strong, Alex," he said, wiping my face with a mucky cloth. He didn't call me Captain Alex. Was Thomas actually softening as well?

For some reason I seemed to trust Thomas more than any of the other pirates.

The rest of the day seemed to take forever to pass. I could not make myself believe that I was going to survive – at this point in my mind there were too many circumstances going against me. I was watching all the pirates for any signs that they were going to follow the plan or not. The light was fading and I became jittery when I heard a boat arrive on the scene. Still in my mind there was the risk they might meet the guys in the boat, kill them, grab the money and kill me, nobody said anything about the ransom handover, it was all very quiet. Eventually Thomas came and gave me the news that the two PW men had arrived at the village and were on their way in the hired boat.

"We will be leaving soon, Alex. Be strong. It will not be long now, you will soon see a doctor," he said.

"Thanks," I croaked pathetically.

About another half an hour ticked by and I heard a boat's engine roaring into action again. Was this it?! Then my heart sank as I heard it leave the creeks and head off into the distance. Oh my God, that is it, they have gone to get the money and they have not taken me. I honestly thought that I was finished, I wondered if Thomas would do me a favour and shoot me quick, I did not want the young pirate to set me on fire. My mind was in a state of shock, I did not know what to do or think at this point. I began to tremble and started to panic. I waited and waited. I did not know what was going to happen at this stage but I wanted to get out of there now. I lay on my makeshift bed and pretended that my body was shaking worse than it actually was. I shouted for help and asked for more water but my cries were ignored, this lack of reaction from any of the pirates did not look good.

After about another 20 minutes or so, Thomas, Nick and two other gang members came in.

"OK, Alex, time to leave. We are going now," said Nick.

Were we actually going to meet my two friends or were the pirates taking me to a secluded spot to kill me?

They picked me up and carried me over the uneven clearing to the bank. Then they passed me down to four more guys in the second boat. They are going to shoot us all in the water, I thought to myself. All the time they were carrying me I was trembling uncontrollably. They must have been very worried, they must have also been wondering if I was going to make it to the meeting place. The engine revved into life and we headed out. I was utterly discombobulated and had no sense of direction. I thought we were heading upstream, in the opposite direction to when we first arrived. We started to pick up speed, and then we slowed down again to clear a narrow channel with overhanging branches. It was very dark now. The guys were periodically sounding the depth of the water with sticks. Then we stopped. Nobody spoke and we bobbed up and down in the water. Suddenly there were cracks of gunfire. Oh my God! The guys in the other boat have killed the messengers, I thought. This was the end I did not want. I was so shocked when I heard the gunshots, my mind was racing with all sorts of thoughts. I felt tears welling up in my eyes, I felt sure at that point that I was going to die, and the thing was, I could do nothing to help myself. My fate was in the pirates' hands.

I learned later that the shots were a signal from the first pirate boat to the second pirate boat that all was clear for us to proceed. After the shots we roared off again and we were soon out in a large bay. I could see some faint lights on the shore in the distance. I was lying with my head on Thomas' shoulder. I was trying to see what the pirates were thinking and trying to figure out what was going on around me. I said to Thomas and Nick, "My heart is weak, I am going to die."

Thomas said, "Alex you are not going to die, it is almost over, you will see a doctor tonight and he will give you drugs."

We powered on for another five minutes with the sea splashing our faces. Then we stopped again. I managed to grab a peek of the other pirate boat. It was alongside another boat which I presumed was the hire boat. I could make out the silhouettes of several people on board. My spirits were raised. Was there now a real chance that I was going to make it out of here alive?

Nick shouted to the other pirate boat and told them to take the hired boat alongside ours. Within minutes, all three boats were alongside each other with the hired boat sandwiched in the middle. There was a lot of shouting, yelling and gesticulating.

It was really dark and the whole scene was lit by the glimmering moonlight. This was a surreal moment. One of the guys gingerly passed over a large plastic bag that had actually been made in Ghana. It was pulled over into the boat I was in. I had seen these type of bags whilst working in Ghana, one of the Ghanaian crew told me that they were strong bags that were exported all over Africa. The guys on our boat were shouting in pidgin English that they were going to count the money. But the pirates on the other boat said they had already counted it and every penny was there. To my astonishment and utter surprise, Thomas helped me to sit up and smiled.

"OK, Captain Alex, we are going to pass you over to your people now," he said.

Was this too good to be true? Why would they pass me over if they were going to kill us? There must be a chance! Maybe they would pass me over and kill us all in the same boat. My mind was racing with all kinds of thoughts. Were these guys going to do the dirty right at the last minute?

I recognised the guys in the boat as Alabo and Omini, two colleagues who I had known for many years. What brave Nigerian friends they were to risk their lives for me. I was lifted up and dangled over the water for a moment, as Alabo and Omini stood up and took a firm hold of me. Thomas and Nick released me very gently, and I was laid down in the hire boat.

"Head back to the village slowly and take it easy as the Captain is very sick," said Nick to the hired boat driver. I was very surprised to hear those words coming from Nick.

I continued to play my part, placing my head on Alabo's shoulder.

"Take good care of him and get the Captain to the nearest hospital as soon as possible."

I could not believe what I was hearing. Nick told the hired boat driver that they would follow us for a short time and then leave us. So we started heading off. I kept looking back in anticipation, expecting them to come after us.

"Don't worry, Cap. You are with us now. You are safe they will not do anything now," said Alabo as he patted me on the head in comfort. Alabo and Omini gave me a hug and said how good it was to have me there safe and sound.

Suddenly, both pirate boats started speeding back towards us. They turned so close and sharply to us that we were all drenched with sea water. I was on edge I thought this was the final showdown scene. They had their money, so why would they turn back towards us? I was waiting for the shots as I lay my head on Alabo's shoulder; I started trembling uncontrollably. The driver and crewman of the boat both ducked down and were also shaking, the only ones that were calm were Alabo and

Omini, they seemed to know that everything was going to be all right. I was not so sure.

"Don't shake, Captain. Everything will be OK," said Omini.

After the boats were very close to us, both boats turned to go back the way they had come and were only a few metres away when both boats slowed down. I looked over and the strangest thing happened, every one of the pirates stood up in the boats and waved to us. Both boats then sped off and disappeared into the darkness. Was it finally over? I asked myself. I was still not sure we were safe.

"They are all mad," said Omini, shaking his head as we started to speed away. This time for good.

"How are you, Captain?" Omini asked.

"I'm not great but I'm not as sick as I was making out," I told him.

I then told him the full story and why I had to feign illness and a couple of heart attacks.

"Well done, Captain," he said.

Both Alabo and Omini were so very happy that I had been released, and it was wonderful to see my Nigerian friends laughing and smiling. I was so immensely grateful for what they had just done for me and told them so. They had left their wives and children, maybe to never see them again, to come to a strange place with a bag full of money to get me out of there. The risks the both of them had just undergone were immense. What would their families have done if they did not return home? I asked them if they were scared and worried about coming here. They both said they did not even think about it. When Chris told them I had been kidnapped and was being held hostage, they volunteered their services immediately. They said that for me they would have done anything. For them to volunteer for this task was amazing. Chris had asked for volunteers and they both stepped forward immediately. This was true friendship and loyalty.

"By the way do you have a cigarette?" I asked Alabo.

"St Moritz Menthol? I bought your kind especially for you," said Alabo.

"That would be great, you are wonderful," I said.

He passed a cigarette to me and lit it. I took a long drag and exhaled a long stream of smoke out into the night. The pirate boats disappeared into the dark distance. Was I safe? I was not at all sure yet. I took another satisfying puff on my cigarette. It tasted so good. The boat speeded up and after what seemed like an eternity we pulled into the village harbour. Enthusiastically I stepped ashore on to dry ground.

Omini recounted what had happened before the transfer and I trembled at the thought of what had gone on earlier. Alabo and Omini had walked from the car park down to the boat pier carrying a large plastic bag full of Naira. They had no escort, all the bush bars and small roadside stalls were thronged with people. What if they had been mugged and the money was stolen, what would have happened to me then? After they hired the boat and reached the rendezvous point in the bay, the first pirate boat came racing towards them. The boat hire man was so scared he soiled himself. He shouted that if he had known he was being hired to do this sort of thing he would have refused. The gunshots we heard were from the first pirate boat, signalling the all clear to come out of the creeks. A couple of the pirates pointed their guns at the water and fired several rounds of ammo. Alabo admitted that when the pirates lifted the guns to shoot into the water he thought they were going to die. The whole episode was fraught with danger.

When the three of us considered the transport of the money from the car to the boat, and then to the handover point, we all realised how lucky we were that nothing had gone wrong. Alabo and Omini said some prayers and thanked the Lord for looking after us. But the driver and crewman of the hired boat were livid with us. They demanded more money than the sum

Omini had initially agreed to pay. They hadn't agreed to be part of such a dangerous job. They did calm down though and I thanked them for what they had done. They were glad I was safe. I also thanked Omini and Alabo for their bravery and for volunteering to come to rescue me.

"Not a problem. For you, we would do it again it," said Omini.

They had both taken an immense risk for me. What would have happened to their families if the outcome had been different? It did not bear thinking about.

Omini and Alabo helped me up the ramp and we left the boat guys with another big thank you ringing in their ears. I limped through the village which was busy with evening activity. Every single eye followed us along the road. Omini stopped a car and agreed to pay the driver to take us to the car park, where they already had a hire car with a driver. He drove us to a second car where we switched again, this time with the hired private police in another car.

The police had escorted Omini and Alabo to this point because the road from Port Harcourt to the village is a notorious hotspot for militants. This was another obstacle that my two friends had to overcome. The road from Port Harcourt to Eket was well known to both Alabo and Omini, there had been several attacks on cars in the past by militants, so they were on edge all the way. They never stopped once. Before they arrived in Eket it was getting dark, so now the police escorts had to be very alert. This journey would be stressful under normal circumstances but the big bag of money they were carrying, that was going to save my life, made the journey even more precarious. The road after Eket to the village where Alabo and Omini had to hire the boat was unknown territory to them both. They could not wait to get to the village, there was still going to be dangers to face but at least the car journey and the dangers that held would be over.

We started our journey north, could I be sure that I was safe, or would something else now emerge?

# 15

# AN EVENTFUL JOURNEY TO LAGOS

The police escort drove off briskly in front of us as we followed. I used to think that an escort was always following behind, but in Nigeria the escort goes first. If there are militants about to ambush they will be deterred by the blue flashing lights. At least that is the theory.

When we were underway, Omini called Chris and told him the good news. I was sitting in the back and he passed me the mobile. It was intensely emotional hearing his friendly voice.

"I'm so pleased to have you ashore and in safe hands," he said.

"You would not believe how good I feel now being able to talk to you as a free man," I replied.

I was now overwhelmed with the whole episode, and tears ran down my cheeks. I could barely speak. I could not believe that I was free.

"Take your time, Alex. I'll call Helen now and tell her you're safe."

"Thank you so much, Chris. For everything you have done for me."

"That's OK. You are very welcome."

He went off and phoned Helen immediately, telling her I had been released and was in safe hands. After days of pent-up worry and emotion, she too was overwhelmed. I later learned that when the news came through, Helen and the police hugged each other. I gather they all had a wee celebratory drink. Helen called Tracey in Brechin at around 8.30pm on the Friday night. She shouted down the phone with euphoria, crying out that I had been released. I was with my own people, the handover had been done, money was exchanged and I was now safe. In disbelief, Tracey asked several times, "Are you sure? Are you sure?" Helen reassured her I was safe and she could stop worrying now her dad was free. Tracey burst into tears with the news. The relief was overpowering. Then her daughter Darcie came in from her work, and asked, "What are you crying for, Mum?" It was then that Tracey could tell her what happened and explained that she wasn't allowed to tell her for my safety. By now, both Darcie and Tracey were crying too. So much emotion just spilled out. Dean came in and he was told the whole story. They all took it well and understood why they had not been told until I was released. They were simply relieved and could not wait to see me home. Tracey called David and let him know. My incredible family were so glad that I was alive and were eager to get me home.

Chris said I should call Helen as soon as possible. She could not wait to hear my voice. That would be the confirmation she wanted. By now, I was so overcome with emotion and relief that everything was a blur.

Alabo had been my driver for a long time and had my home number on his phone. He dialled the number for me. I waited as it connected internationally. Then I heard Helen's voice and I was almost blubber. We both just cried initially. Alabo told me he didn't have much credit on his pay phone, so the call was short and sweet.

"I love you so much and I am so glad you are safe," said Helen.

"I love you very much too. I will talk to you in the morning," I said.

Chris rang again saying I should go straight to the hospital in Eket, which was a quarter of the way up the road, and where Exxon Mobil were based. He was concerned and wanted to get me seen by a doctor as soon as possible. I told him that I would prefer to go straight to Port Harcourt where it would be safer. He agreed and told me that the two South African guys from the insurance company had been with him all day, helping with the release operation. They had all given each other a big hug when Omini confirmed my release and that the handover went well.

They were all so relieved. With his typical dry humour, Chris told me that after the derisory first offer, he had told the South Africans that if I made it home they could expect me to punch him on the chin. I told him that after the first offer he made, I thought that's it, I am definitely dead now. We both chuckled.

About thirty minutes up the road we came to a small village where we stopped to get some water and a pack of cigarettes. Omini asked if I wanted a sandwich. After over four days without a scrap of food I could not eat anything. I just wanted my cigarettes.

Omini and Alabo looked at the insect bites on my arms and legs and they were shocked. My skin was a terrible mess of sores. I felt stinky and filthy. I asked Omini if he could buy me a pair of underpants, a pair of tracksuit bottoms and a T-shirt. It was rather late but if he saw any shops open he would stop. Alabo said if we could not get anything he would go to his house in Port Harcourt and pick up a change of clothing for me there.

When we arrived at Eket the police car indicated to us to pull over. Eket is another place where you have to be very careful, especially at night. There are often militants on the prowl because of the presence of Exxon Mobil. We pulled in behind them, Omini told me to sit tight. Alabo and Omini went to the police car. After about 15 minutes they both returned and we continued the journey.

"What was the problem?" I asked.

"The police did not realise they were going to be working so late and their company would not pay them overtime. They wanted to stay in Eket for the night and continue the journey in the morning," said Omini.

"What did you say?"

"I told them they would get their overtime and a bonus but we needed to get you to Port Harcourt to see a doctor."

Was this ordeal ever going to end? We drove on to Port Harcourt. I asked Omini if it would be possible to go straight to the hotel. I wanted out of those ragged clothes and wanted to soak in a long, hot bath. I would go to the doctors in the morning.

He phoned Chris who insisted we go straight to the company doctor. She was already expecting us. Chris told me that he wanted me in Lagos on the Saturday. There were people waiting to see me, so I had to go to the doctor that night. He needed to know if I would be allowed to or indeed able to fly.

We arrived at the doctor's clinic in Port Harcourt at about 11.30 pm on the Friday evening. It was a small modern office near the centre of the town in a quiet side street. The light was on. Omini took me into the white-washed reception where we checked in. The sleepy-looking receptionist asked me to fill out a form but I explained that I was already registered and was a captain with PW. She found my registration card and told us to have a seat. Ten minutes passed and then the doctor arrived. She ushered me into her consulting room. She was an older Russian lady and had been in Nigeria a long time with her husband, who was also a doctor. She had been forewarned by Chris that I was coming and what had happened. She began her examination, checking my breathing and listening to my heart through her stethoscope.

"You're not looking good, Captain," she smiled. "But we will help you get better. These bites look very sore and tender."

"They are nipping and itching like hell," I grimaced.

"I can see the skin is broken in many places. I will need to take a blood sample to test you for malaria, although I feel sure you are infected with the malaria bug," she said.

"If you can get any out," I replied.

"I will need quite a bit of blood. We will test for malaria, but there are other tropical diseases you might have. There are so many unknown insects in the jungle."

"I think I met them all," I said, trying to make a joke. It didn't work. Perhaps it was too late for her to raise a smile.

She tied a tourniquet around my left arm, dabbed an area with an antiseptic wipe, and then inserted the needle into my arm. It stung a little and then she drew the blood back into the hypodermic syringe.

"We will get the results of the blood tests by noon tomorrow," she said.

She filled five more vials with blood for the various tests and told me that under normal circumstances she would have kept me in overnight for observation. She was going to give me some drugs but I had to eat before taking them. The problem was finding expat food at that time of night. She asked Omini what hotel I was staying in. It was one of the better ones and she said it was probably a better place to relax. She gave me a concoction of drugs and several creams from her cabinet and explained what I had to do. She told me to eat some grilled or boiled chicken and boiled potatoes. Nothing fried.

"Goodnight, Captain. I hope you make a quick recovery from your ordeal," she said.

"Do you think I will be OK to travel to Lagos later today?"

"I have no objections, if you feel up to it. Just remember you are very weak."

"I think I can do it. Thank you so much for your time tonight – and all that you have done for me."

"Thank you. That's my job," she said.

It was about 1am when we arrived at the hotel. It was fully

booked so we went off to find another one. We were lucky, we found a room, and Omini checked me in. He was going to stay in another hotel close by as there was only one room available in the hotel I was in. He was coming back at 8 am and it was about a 2 hour drive to his house, so it was not worth going home. He called his wife and told her everything and that he would see her the next afternoon after I had left. We asked the receptionist if it would be possible to order grilled chicken and boiled potatoes. They could see I was in a terrible state as I still had on the same clothes that I had been wearing for four days in the jungle. They said the food would not be a problem. They would tell the kitchen and the food would be taken to my room in about 40 minutes. I had time for a shower. After which I would try and get a bit of rest.

It was time for Alabo to head off, even though it was late, he went home and got me clean tracksuit bottoms, a football shirt, toothbrush, toothpaste and some more cigarettes and then returned to the hotel. I thanked him from the bottom of my heart. He gave me a massive hug.

"Dear friend, you have saved my life, brought me here to safety and shown me kindness and concern. Thank you so much. Words alone cannot express how grateful I am to you. I will forever be in your debt," I gushed.

He looked very humble and said how sorry he was because of what happened. He wished me goodnight and told me he would see me in a few hours. I wished him goodnight and thanked him again. I also told him to thank his wife for allowing him to do what he did for me today.

I took the stinking clothes off and threw them in the bin. I never wanted to see them again. I turned on the shower which was set into a bath. I had to use the nail brush to remove the embedded dirt from my hands, fingernails and filthy feet. I scrubbed hard. It was painful due to the bites and the broken skin. After 20 minutes, the bathwater was filthy. I let the water out and washed the earthy sediment from the bottom of the bath. After having a shower for about 20 minutes I wrapped the bath towel around me. There was a knock on the door. I answered it, and my food arrived on a tray. The plate was filled with slithers of grilled chicken and a mound of boiled potatoes. I felt sick looking at it. I tried to eat but could only manage a few mouthfuls of potato and a slice of chicken. I then took the drugs as instructed by the doctor washing them down with plenty of bottled water.

I rang room service to get another bath towel and I ran another bath. I soaked in the bath and then had another shower. After I dried myself, I sat on the bed and smoked a couple of cigarettes. How could something like this have happened to me? Life would never be the same again. I did not sleep. I was wide awake and chain smoked for most of the night. There were the stubs of nearly two packs of St Moritz in the ashtray in the morning. Despite the windows being open and a shower of refreshing topical rain it was still very hot and humid. I could hardly breathe, but still the cigarettes were getting smoked rapidly.

At 7am after cleaning my teeth and having another shower, I called room service and ordered a coffee and some toast so that I could take my drugs again as instructed. An hour later, Omini and Alabo arrived in great spirits. Omini joked he would call me Alabo since I was wearing all of his clothes. They both asked how I was bearing up and how it felt to be free. Omini told me that he was going shopping to get me some items for travelling to Lagos. He started to measure me up for a shirt, trousers, socks and shoes. He would also buy me a small travelling bag and a cheap mobile phone. Alabo left me his phone earlier that morning with some new credit so I could call home. Omini also told me that Chris was trying to get me booked on a flight to Lagos at 1pm.

"Captain, you must take it easy but we don't have much time. It will take us an hour to get to the airport, and you must be there one hour before the flight," said Omini.

"What about the blood test results?" I asked.

"Don't worry about that. I can pick them up. Let's just get you on a flight," he said.

They left me, and Chris called. He asked how my night went, I told him that my skin must be washed away but I still felt dirty and that I did not sleep. There was too much on my mind. He said, "Mate, I am not surprised. You have just been through a terrible ordeal."

"Have you spoken to Helen this morning?"

"I'm just about to call her."

"OK, great. We need you in Lagos, are you OK to travel on your own?" Chris asked.

"I'm sure I can manage, the flight to Lagos is only an hour from here."

Chris told me that I was booked on the 1pm flight and we could collect the ticket when we arrived at the airport.

"I'll be there to meet you. Take care and have a safe journey. By the way, how's Omini getting on?"

"He's been brilliant. The guys have both gone shopping for me. I'm so grateful to both of them."

"It's great to have you back safe and a little bit sound, Alex," he said, joking.

We said our goodbyes and I called Helen. It was a very emotional call and we had a bit more time to talk about what had happened. I could sense her relief and happiness. I was indeed safe. She told me what had been going on in Montrose and that the police had just left, but they would return to see me the day after I arrived home. She said she had thanked them very much and could not stress how helpful they had been during this very difficult time. She told me that the family were aware of what had happened and that I had been released. They were shocked and surprised that their mum and grandmother had kept it a secret. When she explained why, they accepted this.

"They are all sending their love to you. And you have to hurry home," Helen said.

"I will. But I can't get an emergency passport until Monday. If all goes well, I will travel on Monday night and be back in Aberdeen on Tuesday morning."

It was around about 11am before Omini and Alabo got back to the hotel. Omini said we did not have much time and that we had to go soon. Alabo and Omini had bought me some quite smart clothes. I applied more cream to the insect bites then both Alabo and Omini helped to get me dressed in my new gear. Omini also gave me a small brief case very similar to a laptop case, in this bag were a toothbrush, some cigarettes, and some small Naira notes, Omini also gave me a new Nokia mobile phone, and Alabo had already punched in some personal numbers that I would need. Omini checked me out and paid for the hotel and we headed for the airport with armed police ahead of us and behind us. When we arrived at the airport Omini and Alabo both came to the ticket collection desk and then the check-in desk with me. After I had my ticket and boarding card to Lagos we had to say our goodbyes. It was very emotional. I gave them both a firm hug.

"I can never thank you enough for what you have done for me. You both put your lives at risk for me. You have shown immense bravery," I said.

"We have always enjoyed working with you, Captain. You have been kind to us. We would not let anyone harm you," said Alabo.

I had a lump in my throat, and I was welling up. I could feel the tears. I'm a strong Scottish seaman who finds it hard to show emotion, yet my depth of feeling and love for these Nigerian guys from a very different and puzzling culture was immense.

"You took all that money through dangerous places to secure my release! You might have been hijacked or killed yourself. Then what would have happened to me, I asked, we

145

would do the same again for you if need be, Captain," said Omini.

I assured them both that there would never be a next time.

We said our goodbyes and I made my way to the departure lounge and sat down. I was glad of the seat as I was still feeling very weak. I kept thinking, am I really here? Am I really free? I did not think I was going to feel 100% safe until I was back home with my wife and family in Montrose, Scotland. Just before the flight was called, Omini called me and said the doctor had stated that there were signs of malaria in my blood but nothing else. The doctor had already given me a large dose of pills to fight the malaria. The flight actually left in good time. After take-off the captain announced that the flight to Lagos would take 50 minutes, arriving ten minutes early.

As announced, we touched down at 1.50pm. I had no bags to collect, so it was just straight out to the meeting point, and standing right at the exit door was Chris. We gave each other a big hug and again it was an emotional reunion.

"It is so good to see you, Alex," Chris said.

"Chris, Thank you. Thank you. I'm delighted to see you. I thought for a while in the jungle that this time might never come."

We walked to the car where the driver was waiting. In the car Chris knew how I felt and that I needed a rest. He told me that I would not meet with the two South Africans from the insurance company until noon the next day. Chris also told me that the PW camp was full of workers but he had not told any of them about my ordeal.

"I'd rather not have everyone scrambling around you and giving you more stress. I think we should get you somewhere a bit quieter," he explained.

We drove to a small hotel where I had stayed before when the camp was full. This hotel was very good, enclosed by a very large wall with armed security guards everywhere. This made me nervous seeing all these guns again but I knew it was for my own safety this time. Chris checked me in and paid for two nights in advance. We sat in the lounge and Chris had a beer while I had a Diet Coke. We had a long chat but Chris tried to avoid going into the gory details. I would have to go through every detail with the South Africans the next day at the debriefing. Chris said goodnight and told me that he would pick me up the next day at 11.30am. I ordered a salad sandwich for tea. I could not eat much as my tummy was still not right, although the diarrhoea had calmed down a lot. The pills were having an effect too. I felt a little bit safer now. I called Helen again and we had another long conversation. I told her more about what had gone on. She cried again.

"I can't wait until Tuesday, until your back home," she said, signing off.

"Goodnight, I can't wait either. Give me a call in the morning. I love you," I said.

Chris also called to see if everything was OK and to say goodnight. He asked if everything was ok and how I was feeling now. I told him that I was improving all the time and felt a good bit better. He assured me that my ordeal was over and told me to relax. I asked Chris how the crew were and if they were all safe. He told me that the vessel was ashore in Calabar now and that all the crew were fine. A couple of them had been bashed about a little during the attack but they were all fine. Chris told me that the crew that had been on board during the attack were all due to go on leave and would be home with their families soon. They had all been asking after me and passed on their best regards. He told me that Captain Bob had returned to take command of the vessel, although Bob had only been on leave for four weeks he did not have a problem returning early.

# 16

# MY THREE SPECIAL FRIENDS AND LIFE SAVERS

When Chris received the call from the base manager, Richard, who had been called by the *Saint Patrick* at 0500 hours on Tuesday the 14<sup>th</sup> of May, Chris was told the vessel had been attacked and his captain kidnapped. He was in a state of shock and he did not want to believe Richard. He asked Richard if his information was true, Richard assured him that it was indeed true. Richard had been told by Erik, the chief officer of the vessel. Richard had asked Erik if he was being serious. Erik told him that he was being deadly serious. Richard informed Chris of what had happened up to now, and that the incident had also been reported to Exxon Mobil. Chris instructed Erik, via Richard, to secure the vessel as best as possible. Chris also enquired about any damage done to the vessel. Erik told Richard that he thought there was a lot of superficial damage but that he did not think there was any serious damage done to the navigation equipment. Chris asked Richard if there had been any instructions given from the pirates and if Erik had any idea where the pirates had taken me. Richard answered no to both questions. Chris told Richard that he would make arrangements for the vessel to be taken to Calabar for repairs and that he would get Captain Bob back, if he agreed of course. Chris then contacted all the authorities. He asked the British High Commission if they would call Helen, they said that

Helen should be told in person and not by phone, and that they would contact London, to send a team from the Scottish police to tell Helen. The police would also stay with her until this was all over. He called Lyn, his wife, to let her know what had happened and Lyn was amazed. She wished Helen all the best and that she should stay strong. Chris said he was in a state of turmoil, not only was I his Captain but I was also one of his best friends. How could this be happening? Chris could not believe that he did not get a phone call from the kidnappers that first day. He was on tenterhooks and did not know what to do. He tried calling both my numbers but at that point the phones were switched off.

When he did receive the call the next day from Nick, he was astonished at the figure the kidnappers were asking for. How could he get his hands on 150 million Naira? He would do anything he could to get me out of there safely. When he talked to me he had to stay strong and although he could hear the anxiety in my voice, he had to reassure me at all costs.

Chris received support from the Scottish police offering him guidance on what to say to the kidnappers. The police also called Chris with the list of drugs that I had been prescribed, so he could pass this information onto the kidnappers. The police connected their phone to his phone, in order to hear what the kidnappers and Chris were saying and to record the conversations.

The day after the attack Chris called Helen, by which time she had been told of the situation by the police He was desperate to talk to her and explain what was going on between the kidnappers and himself. Chris told Helen to be strong and that he would have me back to her soon. He was quite sure that everything was going to turn out fine and that the kidnappers would not hurt me.

Throughout my ordeal and until I was safe, Chris could not sleep nor rest, and he never had one minute to himself. He was so worried about me and he felt so helpless. This was a new thing for him as well. Chris had to look after the vessel and the crew. The crew were obviously severely shocked and wanted to go home. The vessel was badly damaged and had to go to port for repairs. His head was spinning and he did not know if he was coming or going at times. After the first couple of days of my captivity he had the two insurance guys from South Africa to deal with as well. He also had to make sure there was money at hand and ready to go as soon as the kidnappers agreed on a sum. The two insurance guys were advising Chris not to let the kidnappers know how much money he was willing to pay. They told him that if he let them think he had plenty of money, then they would demand all the more.

Adding to the chaos, the Scottish police were also advising Chris what to say to the kidnappers. But his biggest problem was getting his friend out of the jungle and in one piece. How he managed to cope I do not know, but he came through with flying colours. When he had agreed with the pirates the amount of cash that was to be handed over for my release, Chris had to make sure the cash was ready that day and that there would not be any hiccups at the last minute. He had to ask Omini, the company procurement officer and Alabo, my ex-driver, if they would be prepared to take this money to meet the pirates to secure my release. He told them both that they did not have to do this if they did not want to, and that he could try to get someone else if they so wished. But they would not hear of it, and were prepared to do anything for Captain Alex. He knew that this was a big risk. He would have taken the money himself but the insurance company reps and the Scottish police said that under no circumstance could Chris go anywhere near the kidnappers, this would be reckless. If they got a hold of two expats it could spell disaster, and who would deal with the kidnappers if Chris was taken as well? He knew that Omini and Alabo would not have a problem trying to save my life, as the three of us had been very close for many years. I had actually known Alabo a few years longer than Chris had known him. Chris was so worried about the two guys' safety and that of their families should, God forbid, anything happen to my two friends.

From the time Alabo and Omini left Port Harcourt, Chris was trembling with fear, he prayed that everything would run smoothly and the guys would return home with me safe and sound. Whilst the guys were travelling to the village and negotiating the exchange in the hired boat, Chris was talking to the kidnappers. His head was so mixed up with various thoughts he did not know where he was and was functioning on autopilot.

Chris said that when Omini called him to say that everything had went well and they had me in their car, he was so relieved he had to hold back his emotions. The insurance guys were also listening to Omini, and gave out a huge gleeful shout and hugged each other. Chris said, he was so delighted that I was finally free and safe, he could have collapsed with relief. He could not wait to get me to Lagos, and to see me in person again would be a massive relief for Chris.

Chris and I will always remain dear friends. I will never forget what he did for me, he is one of three special people that I owe my life to. After my ordeal I went home and relaxed as best I could. Chris had to stay in Nigeria and face other ordeals – he deserves a lot of praise.

When Chris first told Omini and Alabo that I had been kidnapped they were shocked by the news. Chris told the both of them that there would be a ransom demand at some point, and that he would most likely need someone to go with the ransom money at some stage to secure my release. Straight away they both said that they would go when the time came. Chris said they were adamant that no one else should go and that they would be the ones as they both thought the world of me and would do anything for me. They both told Chris that God would be on their side and that all three of us would be reunited with our families at the end of all this. After they left Chris they both went home and told their wives the story. They told their wives that when the time came, they were going to meet the kidnappers with the ransom money to secure my release. Both of their wives agreed that they were doing the right thing. During the next couple of days Alabo and Omini were calling Chris constantly to find out if he had any news and when they were needed to go with the ransom money.

On Friday the 17th May 2014 Chris called them both to tell them that he had struck a deal with the kidnappers and that they would be travelling with the ransom money that day. He asked them if they were still willing to take this big risk. They both said yes, and the quicker they got on their way the quicker all this would be over and I would be safe. They both went and said goodbye to their wives, who wished them well and God speed. Next they went to the office, and Omini then went to the bank to collect the money before returning to the office. Chris told them to count the money two or three times to make sure every penny was there. He told the two guys to make sure the money was 100% correct when they handed it over to the pirates. Chris was sure the pirates would count the money to the last penny. Chris gave them instructions for the journey and told them not to call my numbers under any circumstances – Chris was the one who would do all the talking to the pirates. Chris made sure they had enough money for expenses and some extra for emergencies. The three of them went through the plan several times until they were all on the same page. Chris had obviously gone through the plan with the guys from the insurance company, and everyone had agreed on what had to be done.

Omini and Alabo left the PW base at 1500 hours with 13.1 million Naira in a large plastic carrier bag. They both wondered how this trip would end and if they would see their families again, but with God on their side they felt sure that everything would go well and they would be travelling back to

Port Harcourt with me later that day. Throughout the journey Chris was calling them both to make sure everything was going to plan. When the pirates called Chris, he would call Omini to pass on the pirates' instructions. Omini and Alabo said the whole journey was nerve-wracking and very stressful. There was an armed police escort in their car and another car with three armed guards in front of them. Obviously they could not make this very dangerous journey with all this money unescorted.

They arrived at the village where they were instructed to hire a boat, they now knew that they were on their own, this was as far as their police escort was allowed to go, as instructed by the pirates. They had to leave the cars about 800 yards from the jetty where they would hire the boat. Now came the worrying part, they had to walk through two crowded villages with all this money with eyes on them from all directions. Their hearts were in their mouths. They saw a guy standing beside a small speed boat and they asked him if he and his boat were for hire. The guy said yes but asked a lot of questions. Alabo told him some lies, he did not like doing this but he said, "Needs must." He told the guy that he was going into the bay to meet some of his family in another boat to pick up some clothes for his children back home. He knew that if he had told the guy the truth he would have run a mile. They managed to board the boat with the bag of money without any mishaps. The driver had a helper with him, another guy from the local village. The guy asked Alabo for instructions, which he gave and they set off. After about 30 minutes they arrived out in the large open bay. Omini asked the driver to slow down and he called Chris. After a short period of time they saw another larger speed boat racing towards them, when the boat approached with about ten pirates standing up with guns in their hands the driver and the crewman of the hired boat almost had heart attacks, and were trembling uncontrollably. Omini and Alabo had to calm them down, the pirates came alongside the hired boat and a couple of the gang held the boats together. One of the pirates asked Omini if he had the money, Omini said yes and was told to hand it over, which he did.

The pirates spilled all the money out onto a dry cover on the bottom of the boat and proceeded to count every penny. After they had counted the money and were happy that it was all there, a couple of the pirates raised their weapons and cocked them. Omini, Alabo and the two crewmen all put their hands on their heads thinking this was the end, then the two pirates fired shots in the air and into the water. Omini said at that point they did not know what was going on, and the four of them were scared stiff.

These were the shots that were obviously the signal to the other pirate boat, which I was on, informing them that the coast was all clear. After some time Omini and Alabo saw us racing towards them, and were relieved when they saw me sitting with the pirates. At this point they were thinking the same as myself, was there the slightest chance that this was all going to end the way we hoped? Was I going to be released and were we all going to make it back to the village safely? When the pirates handed me over and both pirate boats left, Alabo and Omini knew that our ordeal was indeed now almost over. They said they know how Nigerians think and act and they knew that the pirates were going to let us get on our way and that I was now free. However, I was still not sure and was still expecting the pirates to shoot us all. Alabo said to me, "Cap. Relax, you are safe now, nothing is going to happen." Both Alabo and Omini were so relieved that my ordeal was almost over, they both gave me a big hug, at this point we were all crying with relief. When I told them both that I was not as sick as I had been making out, they both smiled and said they knew that I was stronger than the pirates had been telling Chris. They both said in unison "Cap, you did well, congratulations." On the trip back to Port Harcourt Alabo and Omini did not ask too many questions as they knew

I had to relax a bit. They allowed me to rest and smoke plenty of cigarettes; they were both very thoughtful and caring.

Both Alabo and Omini told Chris that when they said goodbye to me at the airport, they knew in their hearts that I would not be back to Nigeria and that the likelihood of seeing me again was very remote indeed. But they said that they were just happy that I was safe and was going to be reunited with my family. They both still speak to Chris constantly and ask how my family and I are getting on. Nobody in Nigeria, apart from Chris, has my new numbers, for obvious reasons. For me not to stay in touch with Alabo and Omini is very difficult indeed, but as I said, Chris passes on messages between the three of us, so at least that is something.

As we all know there is good and bad in all walks of life. I have told stories earlier in this book about certain bad things that have happened in Nigeria; this is not a criticism of Nigerian people but is purely to highlight to readers of this book some of the cultures of Nigerian people. Omini and Alabo volunteered for a very dangerous task and risked their own lives to save mine, which they did not have to do, and indeed were not forced to do. This shows that Alabo and Omini are a special breed indeed. They were not tempted by the large sum of money that they had to carry to meet with my kidnappers. They made sure that every penny went to the kidnappers, even though this sum of money could have made them very rich. They showed that my life was more important than money.

I will never forget what Chris, Alabo and Omini did for me in my moment of need, they saved my life. Myself and my family will be forever grateful.

# 17

# INSURANCE REPS AND HIGH COMMISSIONERS

I did not sleep well the first night in Lagos either. I tossed and turned and found it hard to get comfortable. Every time I drifted off I had horrific nightmares and flashbacks: I was seeing the sledgehammers coming through the toilet door, my prison cell in the jungle, I was seeing the young lad's face as he told me he was going to set me on fire. Needless to say, trying to sleep was almost impossible.

On the morning of Sunday 19th May 2013 I phoned room service and ordered scrambled eggs, toast and coffee. I managed to eat a little bit more than the day before and my stomach seemed to be under control now. I then took my pills then had a shave and a shower. I had plenty of growth on my face and chin. This was the first time I had shaved for some time and my skin was sore and tender. After shaving and showering and getting dressed, I spoke again to Helen and Chris on the phone.

At 11.30am, Chris picked me up and again gave me a big hug. He asked how I was doing. I told him I was getting terrible flashbacks of faces in masks and guns. Chris told me that this was bound to happen and he assured me that it would take a while to get over it. We set off for his office and met Geoff and Pieter, the two insurance company representatives. Although I had never met either of them before they both gave me a big friendly hug. Geoff told me that they were so glad and relieved that I was here safe and sound. The two guys told me it was their duty to debrief me and they had to hear the whole story. They said that I would get emotional and it was only to be expected but all I had to do was stop at any time and take a break if I felt it was all becoming too much.

Geoff knew I enjoyed a smoke and said anytime I wanted a cigarette all I had to do was say and I could go to the yard at the front of the office. I started the story and went through the entire ordeal. They asked me a lot of questions about the state of the vessel when we were attacked, especially questions concerning the security precautions that were taken. They asked me the names of the two watch keepers and if I thought that some of my crew could have leaked information to the pirates. This took over four long and exhausting hours. We stopped several times as Chris and I became wrought with emotion. During the debriefing I told Geoff and Pieter about how I overheard the pirates talking about their next attack on the two Bourbon vessels, this was very important information. Chris knew the managing director of Bourbon in Nigeria and he called him as soon as the debriefing was over.

Afterwards, Geoff and Pieter thanked me very much for my detailed debrief and said they were very sorry for putting me through my nightmare again. Chris took me back to the hotel and we had dinner. Chris stayed with me for a long time, keeping me company but I was now mentally fatigued and desperate to rest. Chris explained that he would pick me up the next morning, Monday, and we would go to the British High Commission.

I had to get an emergency single entry passport to get back home, and I would also have to go through another gruelling debriefing with the embassy's security people. Chris arranged to pick me up at 10am and said that he would book me a business class flight home. If all went well at the high commission the next day, I would be travelling the same night.

I called Helen again before trying to get some sleep. I dozed off for a spell and was awoken by recurring nightmares which brought me out in cold sweats. The next morning I had the same breakfast of scrambled eggs, toast and coffee. I then took my pills and had a shower. Chris picked me up and we had quite a long drive to the British High Commission, outside the main city of Lagos on Victoria Island. When we arrived at the gate of the British High Commission, the security people were expecting us and opened the gate immediately. There was a member of the British embassy staff there to meet us. After introducing himself, he took us upstairs and introduced us to another four people, two ladies and two gentlemen. One of the men was a senior police officer based in the British embassy. The first thing we did was fill in some forms for the passport and they took a photograph. I asked them about not having my visa, they said that the immigration officers at the airport were aware of the situation and that I would not have a problem. They gave Chris a number to call in case we encountered any problems at the airport.

While waiting for the passport I was debriefed again, mainly by the police officer, he also wanted to hear everything that I had told Geoff and Pieter. Anything I could tell them that could prevent this happening again would be a great help. He told me there had been a lot of kidnappings in Lagos in the previous few months, involving victims from various countries.

"Are you looking for the guys who kidnapped me?" I asked.

"That would really be a waste of our time," he replied. "We would never find them in that vast jungle."

"So what is being done to protect British workers in Nigeria?" I asked, rather agitatedly.

"There's nothing more that can be done. The fact is that Nigeria has become a dangerous place to live and work," he replied.

Chris had said that he was basically on his own during the period of my captivity, apart from the help he had received from the two South Africans. But of course we must not forget about the Scottish police and the wonderful job they did back home with Helen during my time in captivity. They were marvellous and both Helen and I cannot thank them enough, each and every one.

After the debriefing we sat downstairs and waited for the lady to come down with the passport. After four hours, the lady arrived with the passport. She apologised for the delay, she wished me all the best, gave me a hug and told me to have a safe journey. On the way back to the hotel, Chris said someone had suggested that I should not be allowed to travel home alone. I said I would manage, as I knew he had a lot on his mind and plenty of work to catch up on. Captain Bob had arrived back and the vessel was on her way to Calabar. However, he decided that I should not travel on my own, and called the office and told them to book him a business class flight to Aberdeen with me that evening. Within half an hour his flight had been booked and we had two seats together. He told me he would pick me up at 7pm for our 21.30 departure. I asked him if he was sure about coming, he said, "Absolutely no problem." Back at the hotel I had a bite to eat and took my pills.

# 18

# HOME TO ABERDEEN AND MY FAMILY

My travelling companion, Chris, collected me at 7pm. He settled the bill and checked me out. We made our way to the airport, and when we arrived Chris told his driver that he would be back on Wednesday or Thursday and that he would call him. He called the base manager and gave him instructions on what he had to do. We went to the check-in desk, got our boarding cards and immigration and customs cards. We then went to the business class security control section where we went through immigration and custom control without any problems. We then headed for the business class lounge. I called Helen for the last time before the flight to Amsterdam. At 21:30 hours our flight was called and ready to board. We boarded the flight then sat down and made ourselves comfortable. I now felt safe and that my ordeal would soon be over. I was now overwhelmed with tiredness and close to tears.

I risked a small glass of champagne to celebrate my freedom. Just after take-off the Captain made an announcement that the weather was good and that we would land on time in Amsterdam. The flight went well. The food was excellent although I could not eat very much. I took my pills and tried to read a magazine. But the words were all a blur. I tried to get some rest but dozed for just short periods. An hour before we arrived, the cabin crew came round with breakfast, tea and coffee. I managed some and again took my pills. My stomach was in a lot better shape now, but I was still going to the toilet often. We landed on time in a drizzly Amsterdam. I was glad to be back in Europe. We passed through immigration and customs and headed for the business class lounge. We had a two-hour wait before our flight to Aberdeen was due to board. Chris set up his laptop and checked his emails, and found that there was plenty to do. I went to get us a glass of orange juice and a cup of coffee. When I returned he was still on his laptop typing away furiously. I borrowed one of Chris's phones and called Helen. I told her that all was going well, and that we would be landing in Aberdeen on time at 10am. Helen said she was looking forward to seeing me, and I told her the same.

Chris called Lyn, his wife, and told her that he may fly home from Aberdeen that day and spend a day with her and then fly back to Nigeria. He said he would have a better idea once he arrived in Aberdeen. Lyn passed on her regards. I had talked to Lyn on the phone several times but had never met her. As the flight was called for boarding, I thought, *My God, I am going to be in Aberdeen in one hour and thirty minutes, and an hour's drive after that I will be home. I must be safe now.*

On the flight to Aberdeen we had a coffee and Chris wanted a chat.

"Alex, I know now is not a good time but we have to talk," Chris said.

He told me that I had to go home and relax and that I had to go to see my doctor to get something to help me sleep and calm me down. He told me that Captain Bob had agreed to stay as long as I wanted but that he could not stay indefinitely.

"Take about eight to ten weeks off and don't think about work. After that we will need a decision on whether you want to remain as captain of the *St Patrick*."

"I really need to discuss everything with Helen before I make any major decisions," I told him.

"Certainly. If you decide not to come back we will understand completely, but I will have to find a new captain to go back-to-back with Bob."

It was too soon to make a decision, I needed time to think this all through. I could not tell him what I was going to do but the way I felt right there and then I did not think I could ever go back to Nigeria. This once-in-a-lifetime experience was once too often. I would never want to go through that again. He nodded in agreement. The fasten seat belt signs came on and the pilot told everyone to return to their seats, we would be touching down in Aberdeen in 15 minutes.

I had to convince myself that we really were arriving in Aberdeen and it wasn't just a dream. Chris must have read my thoughts.

"Almost there, mate, this will be very emotional for you all but please be strong," Chris said.

Fifteen minutes later we touched down in Aberdeen, and I felt the tears welling up in my eyes once again. After landing we were directed to the passport checkpoint. When it came to my turn I handed over the emergency single entry passport. The immigration officer must have been forewarned of my arrival. He told me that he had to take the temporary passport from me and that I should apply for a new one. Then, to my surprise, he said in his North-East accent, "It's good to have you home safe and sound, sir." I felt like bubbling again, I thought this was very nice of him. After all he didn't even know me. As we had no luggage, Chris and I went straight to the exit door. Helen and my daughter Tracey were standing there waiting for us. Helen ran to my arms and we hugged each other for ages. There were massive tears of joy and elation. Tracey was also crying and grabbed me around the neck and head to give me a big hug and a kiss. It was so beautiful to eventually see my family again. I introduced Chris to Helen and Tracey. They both gave Chris a huge hug and they thanked him very much indeed for all the help and hard work he had done to get me released and home safely. He told them that the main thing was that I was home now and safe, they also thanked him for travelling with me. He said it was the least he could do.

Chris then said that we should go home and relax, and Helen asked Chris if he was coming home with us for a coffee. He was welcome to stay the night with us if he wished. He was pleased by the offer but he was going to hang around the airport hotel for a while. He told Helen that he had an appointment to meet up with a member of Police Scotland, called Philip Lamb. Philip was one of the officers who had stayed with Helen throughout her ordeal. Chris also said he was going to fly to Norwich the following day and spend a night with his family before travelling back to Nigeria. Chris had been through a lot as well and needed to wind down. I gave Chris another massive hug and again thanked him.

After arriving home I told Helen that I would have a shower before trying some lunch. I had a shave and a shower and put on a clean T-shirt and tracksuit bottoms. I then went to the sitting room and fell into my easy chair. All the strength drained from me. The adrenalin that had kept me going had wiped me out. It was sheer relief and the fact that I was actually home and my ordeal was over. But mental suffering of a completely different kind was only just beginning.

Helen explained that Audrey, one of the police officers that had lived with her for four days, was going to come to see me tomorrow. She also said how difficult it was not being able to tell the family when she received the news that I had been taken hostage, but she did say the family understood why she could not tell them after she explained what the police had said. I went to have a lie down but only slept for maybe thirty minutes. I was experiencing terrible flashing images and all I could think of were the masked faces and guns. I was wondering when and if it would get easier to rest and when

I would at last be able to relax a little. We spent the rest of the day trying to relax, just sitting together and holding each other. Helen said we would not discuss the incident at all that day but watch TV. All she said was, "You did not think you were going to be here but you are, so try to relax and just say to yourself you have a second chance in life." I have heard this statement several times now especially when I'm feeling down it gives me the kick up the backside that I sometimes need. Helen asked if I would like a brandy, she said maybe one or two brandies and Diet Cokes would help me get some sleep that night. I told her I still had a couple of days of my pills to go and that I should not drink until after that. Although we seldom drink and never go to a bar, we do enjoy a brandy and Diet Coke together now and again. The next morning there was a knock at the door and it was Audrey, the Police Scotland officer. Audrey told me how worried everybody had been, especially Helen. She asked me if I was bearing up, and I said that I felt a bit better and a lot safer now that I was home in my own house. Audrey said that she did not want to talk about my ordeal that day as I was just home. Helen made the coffees and I went for a cigarette until the coffee was made. We talked about Helen's and the police officers' time together during my ordeal, and they said how it was a very difficult time for all concerned. Audrey told me that they had been calling Chris three or four times a day for updates, and Chris was also calling Helen and the police when he could. Helen and Audrey talked about Helen making her shopping list and the police going shopping when Helen was not feeling up to it. We had a little chuckle about this. They also spoke about Helen having a police voice recorder just in case the kidnappers called her. Audrey also told me that Helen had been versed on what to say if the pirates did call her.

After a good long chat, Audrey asked if it would be OK for her and her colleague Philip Lamb to come and see us for the

164

debriefing. She was sorry that I would have to go through it again but it had to be done. I may have some things to say that may help them in any similar incidents in the future. I told her that it would not be a problem so we arranged to meet at our holiday home in Arbroath on the Tuesday of the following week. Before she left, Audrey told me to make an appointment with my GP to get checked out again to make sure that my immune system was ok and that my blood was clear of foreign bodies.

Helen suggested we go to our holiday home in Arbroath, as she thought we would get peace there and nobody would bother us. I agreed so we packed a few things and got ready to leave. Just before we left Tracey called and said the grandchildren were desperate to see me.

"Dad, you know the kids will want to know the story. I want to hear it as well, we all want to know and understand what you went through," said Tracey.

When we arrived at the holiday home June was waiting for us. We gave each other a big hug, again this was very emotional. June said she was very sorry for what had happened and that she was glad I was finally safe at home.

The flashbacks were still very vivid I was seeing the faces and the guns as if they were there right in front of me, sleep was still very hard to come by.

On the Saturday, Helen and I went to see Tracey and the kids. David, Dean and Darcie all cried when they saw me. All of them gave me very big hugs. Tracey made us coffee and we all sat in her living room. I went through my whole ordeal from start to finish, which took a long time as the kids were asking loads of questions as we went through the story. I also needed a few cigarette breaks at the back of the house. When I finished the entire story we all had a family hug and cried. The consensus was that I had better not go back to Nigeria. I assured them that I did not wish to go through that ordeal again. The doctor had given me some tablets to try to make me relax and some sleeping pills, but the flashbacks and memories were so bad that the pills were not having the desired effect.

On the following Monday, Helen decided that a shopping spree to replace my jewellery items that were stolen by the pirates may be a good thing for me. Shopping therapy she called it. As it was only about three weeks to my birthday it was a nice idea. We went to the jewellery shops in Arbroath and Helen bought me a new watch. The one I lost was an expensive limited edition Jaguar racing team watch that Helen bought me whilst we lived in Spain; obviously there was no replacing this. However, the one she bought me was a very nice replacement. Helen also bought me a new wedding ring and a new gold neck chain. Helen said that I should wait a while to see if we could get another chain with a Masonic pendant. A few days later I understood why she had suggested this. Helen, Tracey and the grandchildren had bought me a Masonic pendant and a new gold chain with lots of other items for my birthday.

# 19

## DEBRIEFING WITH THE SCOTTISH POLICE AND A LONG ROAD TO RECOVERY

We were still at our holiday home on Tuesday 28th May, when there was a knock at the door. Helen answered, it was Audrey and Phil Lamb, the Scottish police officers, whom I was meeting for the first time. They both shook my hand and said how nice it was to see us both and that they were just sorry it was under very difficult circumstances. Helen made the coffee, once again, and we all sat down. Phil explained that they were going to debrief me. Phil and Audrey said that they would have to go through the whole story from start to finish, but if at any time it was getting too much for me we could stop. They also said that I could have as many cigarette breaks as I wanted

Phil switched on his voice recorder. He said that this was a requirement for the report, and I told him that it was not a problem. Phil and Audrey were both taking notes as well.

We started recalling my ordeal from the day before the pirates attacked, and we continued for about half an hour before I needed to take a cigarette break. After the break we continued for another half an hour and then took another break. I had another cigarette and Helen made some sandwiches for lunch. We continued the story after lunch, and as we were going along Phil and Audrey were asking lots of questions which meant it took a very long time. We got to the point in the story where

Chris had sent the text to the pirates listing the drugs that I was on. I was very surprised when Phil told me that they had instructed Chris about the drugs. Phil actually went to my GP and got a list of the drugs I was on, and then sent Chris the list by text. It was then that Phil wondered if I had picked up on the fact that Chris was emphasising the drug issue. He said although we were thousands of miles apart, he was sure that there was some sort of telepathy between us. He said it was as if I knew what everybody was trying to tell me. I told Phil and Audrey what Chris had told me, and what he said when the pirates told him I was very sick and that I had had a heart attack. Chris had told me in Lagos that he was surprised when he was told I was going downhill so quickly, as he always thought I was very strong; the part about the heart attack really shocked him until he thought about it. He had even said to the two guys from the insurance company at the time, "I wonder if Alex is playing to the crowd here? I know for a fact he is very strong and he seems to have gone downhill very quickly indeed." Phil and Audrey both said it was all making sense now and they were amazed. It looked like we were all on the same wavelength at that time. We had another break and then continued again. The whole thing took us about four hours, and by the end of it all I felt exhausted. Phil and Audrey thanked me and said how sorry they were that the attack and kidnapping had ever happened, and how glad they were that I was home safe. I thanked them both for what they had done for Helen, and Helen thanked them again as well. The day after the police visit, Helen and I went to the shops and then went to the local café for a coffee. Helen said it was not a good idea to mope about the house and that I should get out and about to try to take my mind off of things.

I called my brother Roy and his wife Evelyn. They had no idea what had happened and could not believe it when I told them the basic story. They were shocked and asked me how I was coping. My brother asked why it had not been on the TV or in the newspapers. I told him that the Scottish police said it would only be made public if and when I wanted it to become public. Nobody wanted the press and TV coming to pester Helen and me at this stage. This was to protect us. My brother suggested we pack a bag and spend some time with them at the weekend. So we tried to relax for the rest of the week and then on the Friday packed a couple of bags, got everything together for the two dogs, put the dogs in the jeep and headed north-east. The drive was about one hour and thirty minutes to Oldmeldrum, north-east of Aberdeen. We stopped half way for the dogs and ourselves to stretch our legs. When we arrived at my brother's it was very emotional indeed. They both could not believe what had happened and what I had been through. We all hugged each other and both of them again asked how we were coping. My brother said that there is always a risk in Nigeria of attacks and kidnappings, but he thought as I was captain of a vessel in the Exxon Mobil field with lots of security around that I would be safe. I repeated my story again. My brother is an ex-Royal Marine and he said that if he had been told on the first day of my ordeal he would have jumped on a plane and come looking for me. He was very concerned that the Nigerian government had done nothing to try to help me during my ordeal or to help my company in securing my safe release. The next day he browsed the internet and found a tiny article that stated the St Patrick had been attacked by Nigerian pirates. There was nothing at all about the captain being kidnapped and being held hostage. He felt sure that the British and Nigerian governments were trying their best to keep the whole thing quiet and hushed-up. I agreed with him.

My mum is now 86 years old and we were all worried how the story would affect her; I wondered if she should be told at all. Roy felt she should and said she would be fine as she is a strong lady. I told Roy that I did not think I was strong enough yet, so he agreed to call her. We stayed for four days and Roy and Evelyn were a great help. They seemed to know all the right things to say and do. We had to get home on the Tuesday as I had a doctor's appointment on the Wednesday. Just before we went home, Helen and I went to Roy's local shopping centre and Helen bought me a new laptop to replace the one stolen during the attack. I was grateful to both my brother and his wife for their support.

Chris called every day to see how we were getting on. He told me that the vessel was now in Calabar for repairs. All the broken glass and smashed doors were fixable. We were fortunate that the pirates had not damaged any of the navigation equipment. This would have been very expensive to replace. It was bad enough, Chris said, but it could have been worse

I went to see my GP again and she gave me stronger tablets to help me relax and to help me sleep. She said that it would take a long time to come to grips with what had happened and suggested that I see a counsellor. I agreed and she told me she would make an appointment for me. She gave me a sick note for three months.

As I still had four weeks left of my trip to go when I was kidnapped, I was shocked at the end of the month when I was only paid until the day I arrived home. I spoke to my MD about this. He apologised but it was the way PW worked. Because I was on a day rate I only got paid for the days I worked. I was surprised to say the least.

About a month after my return, Chris called with some news. He told me that the same group of pirates that had attacked the *St Patrick* had attacked two Bourbon vessels. These were obviously the vessels that the pirates had discussed in the jungle, the ones that I told Chris and the two insurance guys about at the debriefing. Bourbon is a French-operated company and for some reason are allowed by Exxon Mobil to carry armed guards on board. When the two small boats laden with pirates came alongside the two Bourbon vessels, they were confronted with armed guards on the decks. A gunfight ensued and seven of the pirates were killed. Although I had a terrible time in the jungle, it did not please me to hear that seven of them had been killed. None of the armed guards on the vessels were killed, nor were any of the crew killed or injured. Chris said that it was down to the information I had given earlier that this attack failed. Helen and I discussed what I should do in the near future. She was adamant that I would not be going back to Nigeria and that we would manage. I told her that we should not make any big decisions yet. After eight weeks, Chris called and asked how I was doing. I told him that things were a bit better but even with the pills I was still not sleeping and still getting very bad flashbacks. Chris said that he did not want to push me but Bob had been on board for eight weeks now and he had to have my decision as to whether I was going to return to the vessel or not. If I was not going to go back then Chris would have to start looking for a replacement for Bob now as it could take quite a while. I told Chris that Helen and I had both decided I was not going back to Nigeria. Chris said he was very upset that I had made that decision but that he understood fully. He said if I changed my mind in six months he would make my job available. He wished me all the best and said we would forever be friends.

Helen and I decided that I would take at least four months off before even thinking about other work. Although I was positive that I would never return to the sea, perhaps I could look for a job onshore. We decided to move house to somewhere quieter. The house in central Montrose would always be a reminder of my ordeal. We moved to a farmhouse in the country just a mile outside of Montrose towards Forfar, Angus. Amazingly, this was the same house that we had lived in 15 years earlier before our move to Spain. It was good to be back, we still had the same neighbours and the remnants of my old fish pond was still there, I re-established the pond and restocked it with some lovely fish, returning it to its former glory. This kept me busy and was very satisfying. Phil

Lamb and I still talk regularly on the phone and send e-mails backwards and forwards quite regularly. We also meet now and then, both of us travelling to various locations to keep in touch. It was during one of our meetings that Phil introduced me to a wonderful guy called Roger Hunt, who was one of the survivors from the horrible attack by terrorists at a hotel in Mumbai, India. Roger has written a book on his ordeal called *Be Silent or Be Killed* and Roger too has become a very dear friend. Phil and Roger have both been instrumental in my recovery, and inspired me to write this book.

After a couple of months in the farmhouse, Helen and I decided that because I was out of work we would give up the farmhouse and go to live in our holiday home in Arbroath. Although my ordeal will never be forgotten it was becoming easier to deal with because of the support I was receiving from Helen, family and friends. The flashbacks were still vivid, but were becoming easier to deal with. After a couple of months at home, my kidnapping became public knowledge, and national and local newspapers ran the story. This was done with my consent to inform people of the dangers they could face if they decided to work in Nigeria. In June 2013 I appeared on a BBC Radio Scotland program called *My Moment Of Fear* which ran for 6 weeks with a different subject each week. I was on the first program which lasted for 35 minutes. It was not easy telling my entire ordeal again to three strangers, but again I did this to let people know exactly how terrifying my ordeal was and how I was sure I was going to die. The three people who were in attendance for the recording of the program were very understanding and patient.

In the months that followed, although I would never forget my terrible ordeal in Nigeria, my life was improving, and thanks to the help of my family and friends, I was beginning to cope a lot better.

In July 2014 I went to help a friend run his trout farm. In

return I can fish when I want for free and it means my friend can relax a bit and concentrate more on his family farm. This has helped me tremendously. After a few weeks at the trout farm, Helen told me that she saw a big difference in me, in my attitude and my demeanour. She said that I actually looked quite happy with life and did not seem so disturbed. She hadn't wanted to say too much before now but she had been very concerned about me when I first came home as I was very quiet, moody and withdrawn. She said that she understood that what I went through was not easy and would indeed affect me for some time, but that I did not seem to be the same man she had known and loved for 36 years. Helen also felt that when I was coming home after the counselling sessions I seemed to be even more depressed and quieter, and she wondered if the counselling was actually a hindrance rather than a help to my recovery. I was not sure in my own mind if the counselling was helping or not, as every time I went to the counsellor it was a case of repeating the story over and over again. At the time this was not what I wanted and seemed to be keeping the memories very fresh in my mind. After several appointments I stopped the counselling and decided to try to cope with things in my own way. Helen said that my daughter and grandchildren had made comments as well to her that they were worried about my condition. They obviously did not want to say anything to me but would tell Helen. Although Helen and the family understood what I had gone through, they wanted the old me back. They all said that the trout farm seemed to be better therapy for me than the counselling. I said to Helen that it was hard to put into words how I was feeling after I came home, I tried as best I could to put my ordeal out of my mind and also tried not to let it affect our relationship but it was difficult at times. It did not matter how hard I tried to put what happened to the back of my mind, I was still tormented by the horrible dreams and flashbacks. Helen understood entirely, but I had to remember that I was at home now with family and friends and that the pirates could not harm me anymore, and that it was in the past.

What I had to remember was that Helen had been through an ordeal as well. From the time she was told of my abduction to the present day, Helen went through something that no wife should have to go through. Even after I arrived home, Helen had to deal with my moods and change in personality, whilst still dealing with the emotional fallout she had suffered after my kidnapping. Helen has been my rock but there have been times when everything has gotten on top of her and she has broken down. Although she tries to be strong for my sake, I have to remember that she has feelings as well and has to be treated with tender love and care.

Helen actually told me that during the time I was being held hostage, she was not expecting me to come home. I had been in Nigeria for 11 years and during this time Helen had learned quite a lot about Nigeria and its culture. She said that if the police had not been with her during that period she may have gone crazy, and is not at all sure if she could have handled the situation on her own. Helen has had to go through lots of different emotions since I arrived home but has somehow managed to prioritise my recovery over her own feelings. Helen is one wonderful lady and a special human being.

# 20

# LIFE GOES ON

It is now December 2014 and I feel at ease with life at last, my terrible experience was something I will probably never forget but with the help of Helen, my family and very good friends I can now look forward.

I am still at the fish farm and it is doing well, this keeps my friend happy, and it is also a big help to me as it prevents me from dwelling on the past. All the customers know the basics of my story and are very good and helpful. I am at the fishery every day during daylight hours, and Helen often comes to the fishery with meals for me. Since I came to the fishery I have taught Helen to fly fish, she enjoys it a lot and wonders why she has never done it before. I fish when I can as well, so we are spending some time together when Helen is not working at the Asda café. In the past year or so I have visited the Police Scotland headquarters with Phil Lamb two or three times to attend negotiator courses. The students are all police officers specialising in negotiating and I have been to the courses to retell my story and to try to help the students understand how a victim feels. The organisers of the course like to get actual victims to give a talk at the courses, to remind the officers that there is always a real life victim in every case they are involved in. When telling my story at each course, I could see that the police officers were engrossed with my story. Throughout my speech, the officers and instructors would ask questions, and I was always allowed to fully answer the question before another question was asked. Phil would always be sitting beside me in case the situation became too much for me, and he also occasionally helped me to answer the questions when needed. At the end of each course all the students would come and thank me personally for coming quite a distance to attend their course. They all said that my story was shocking and amazing at the same time, and they appreciated that recounting my story could not be easy for me. I was told how well I had done and that they would never forget me, they also said how helpful my story was to them.

After the attack on the vessel, the *Saint Patrick* and the PW office in Port Harcourt were sold to a Swedish company operating in Nigeria. Chris has now left PW and is working with another company in Lagos, Nigeria. Chris was made redundant, so therefore had to seek employment elsewhere. Chris has now been with his new company for several months and is enjoying the new challenge. The only drawback is that he has to spend more time away from home, as the company was struggling slightly. Chris got the job of putting the company to rights, which he has done with great success. Obviously this change was quite an upheaval for him as he had to move house in Lagos. He was living in a PW house and he has now moved to another house closer to his new office, which belongs to the company he is working for now. We keep in touch all the time and we pass on each other's news. Omini and Alabo are still doing the same job but with the company that bought the *Saint Patrick* and the PW office in Port Harcourt. They still live with their families in Port Harcourt. They are both doing well and often ask Chris how I am doing and pass on their best wishes. I have to rely on Chris to find out how Omini and Alabo are doing – after the attack I was advised not to give my new telephone numbers to anyone in Nigeria, so Alabo, Omini and I cannot keep in touch by phone.

Capt. Robert Hales, my back-to-back at the time of the attack, contacted me with some shocking news. He told me that the *Saint Patrick* had been attacked again, in a similar location to the last attack. The man who was once chief officer of the vessel (Max from Poland) had been captured by pirates – allegedly the same pirates who had kidnapped me. He was on board the pirate's boat and the Exxon Mobil security vessel had intercepted the pirate boats and started firing shots at them. Max managed to dive into the water and started to swim away. The pirates fired shots at Max in the water but luckily he survived unhurt. He was picked out of the water by the Mobil security vessel and transported back to his vessel – a very lucky escape indeed. It has been said that some of the pirates were killed by the security vessel, but there has been nothing on the news or the net.

To this day I still feel that although I experienced the brutal side of life in West Africa, I had been lucky to experience compassion and kindness also.